TIM, THIS WAS MY
FATHER'S AND I
WOULD LIKE YOU TO
HAVE IT.

REGARDS B[illegible]

The BOB CHARLES
Left-hander's Golf Book

The BOB CHARLES Left-hander's Golf Book

BOB CHARLES
with JIM WALLACE

ANGUS & ROBERTSON PUBLISHERS

*Unit 4, Eden Park, 31 Waterloo Road,
North Ryde, NSW, Australia 2113, and
16 Golden Square, London W1R 4BN,
United Kingdom*

*First published in Australia
by Angus & Robertson Publishers in 1985
First published in the United Kingdom
by Angus & Robertson (UK) Ltd in 1985
First published in New Zealand
by Reed Methuen Publishers Ltd in 1985*

*Published by arrangement with
Reed Methuen Publishers Ltd*

*National Library of Australia
Cataloguing-in-publication data.*

*Charles, Bob, 1936-
The left-hander's golf book.
ISBN 0 207 15158 X.
1. Golf. I. Wallace, Jim. II. Title.
796.352'3*

Printed by Kings Time Printing Press Ltd, Hong Kong

Contents

Acknowledgements

The preparation of this book has been something of an international team effort, with people in many parts of the world providing ideas, help and assistance.

To the following we wish to express our thanks: Jack Nicklaus and Ken Bowden (USA); Volker Krajewski (Switzerland); Ivor and Phyl Charles (New Zealand — Bob's parents); also Roger P. Ganem who assisted with my first book.

Photographers, Peter Bush of Wellington and Harry Ruffell of Christchurch; Kelly Griffiths, Public Affairs Manager, BP (New Zealand) Ltd for library services; Air New Zealand and Shell for library services, and Robyn Hewitt of Wellington, who now admits to understanding how to swing a golf club after typing the manuscript several times.

Special thanks also go to our respective wives, Verity and Jill, for allowing kitchen and dining room tables and sitting room floors to be invaded with photographs and diagrams for weeks while we pondered over the material.

Thanks are also extended to Bob's home club, the Christchurch Golf Club, for making the course available for photographic purposes.

To the many others who offered ideas, we thank you all.

Bob Charles *Jim Wallace*

Dedication

This book is dedicated to the wonderful game of golf, and in particular to all left-handers.

It has been estimated that 10 to 15 per cent of the world's population is left-handed. With many millions of them playing the Royal and Ancient game, those who hit the ball from the other side represent a formidable number on the fairways and greens all over the world. New Zealand, Bob Charles' native country, is said to have the highest proportion of left-handers among registered players of any of the major golfing nations — 10,000 among just over 100,000.

The United States has 14 million golfers, eight per cent of whom play on the left side. Japan is another great golfing nation with more than 14 million players; the number of left-handers, however, is unknown. Lefties are also to be seen in large numbers in Great Britain, Ireland, Australia and Canada.

We hope that all those lefties will gain something from the technical detail in this book. The biographical chapters will show the kind of results that can be achieved through dedication and practice.

It used to be fashionable to switch left-handers to the other side of the ball. Walter Hagen and Ben Hogan are said to have started golf as lefties. But there is no need for change today as instruction and equipment are available. Lefties can play the game as well, and at times better, than others.

Enjoy the book.

Bob Charles *Jim Wallace*

Foreword by Jack Nicklaus

BOB CHARLES may swing from the "wrong" side of the ball as most golfers see it, but don't let that fool you. Bob is an extremely fine player — certainly the best to come out of New Zealand, and for many years consistently one of the best in the world. He's won just about everywhere the game is played, and I still have vivid memories of at least a couple of those victories.

In 1963, at Royal Lytham and St Annes, I finished with a dumb bogey to miss a play-off for the British Open by one stroke, still one of my most painful golfing experiences. The next day Bob won the championship over 36 holes by eight strokes from Phil Rodgers. Day in and day out, Bob at that time was probably the finest putter in the game, and he rolled the ball phenomenally to beat Phil. He also putted superbly when he got me again, by two shots, with a final round of 66, in another national championship, the 1968 Canadian Open at St. George's in Toronto.

But, don't let the heavy emphasis on this part of Bob's game fool you. Before anyone can putt they have to get to the green, and Bob Charles at his peak was just as skilled at doing that as he was once he arrived there. He may not have won many long-driving contests, but he also missed very few fairways and greens, which, in the final analysis, is the key to this game for every golfer.

The reason in Bob's case has nothing to do with which side of the ball he stands, but everything to do with his method and his intelligent, well-controlled, well-paced approach to golf. Right from the start he built an economical, uncomplicated golf swing around solid fundamentals. This enabled him to repeat a predictable pattern of shots with great consistency and confidence.

Also, on the course he has always used his mind ahead of his muscles, which is probably the single biggest challenge the game poses. The result may not always be as visually spectacular as the more go-for-broke type of player, but as the record book shows, it's an extremely successful combination.

Bob and I started out in professional golf at about the same time and have been good friends all along the way. Like me, he's not the flamboyant type, and like me, this has at times given the public a wrong impression of what's going on inside. I know Bob Charles as a warm, responsive and very down-to-earth fellow with a delightful sense of humour, and I wish him well both with this fine book and in all his future endeavours on and off the golf course.

Jack Nicklaus

North Palm Beach,
Florida,
1985.

All lefties: with my parents Ivor and Phyllis.

Introduction

Charles the man

PLAYING golf "on the other side of the ball" — in other words, left-handed — has aroused considerable discussion over the years. Much has been written to suggest that left-handed play would impede a player's development.

Why that should be so baffles me.

For me, playing golf as a leftie is perfectly natural. My parents are both left-handers and enthusiastic golfers. As a toddler I played around with their clubs and a tennis ball in our garden in the small New Zealand township of Hinekura, where dad was the local schoolmaster.

But even before this I had been introduced to the Royal and Ancient game. My mother and two of her friends would take me with them when they played the course at Hinekura. There were nine holes on this primitive course carved out of bumpy paddocks. The three women would heave me and my carriage over the fences (which kept the sheep off the greens) and across the rough ground.

My mother Phyllis was a good golfer, getting down to a 6 handicap at her peak, and her hard work at the game reaped rewards with representation for the Province of Canterbury after we moved to live in Christchurch. Dad was no slug either, getting down to a 2 handicap and collecting numerous district titles. Both my parents still play and I enjoy getting out with them during my annual visits to New Zealand.

With such enthusiastic parents, I suppose it was only to be expected that I should develop a keen interest in the game at an early age. But soon I became interested in other sports, especially rugby football until at the age of twelve I was injured in a game,

With a driver at the age of two.

Signing an autograph after my 1954 New Zealand Open victory.

With a youthful wave I set off from New Zealand in 1961 to embark on my professional career.

and golf became my number one sport. In summer I played cricket.

I worked hard at my golf game, won some trophies and was down to a scratch handicap by the time I was sixteen.

In 1954 I entered and won the New Zealand Open, beating the great Australian Peter Thomson. He had won three years out of the previous four. I was on cloud nine.

With the New Zealand Open victory, I received a lot of media attention. Here is what the *New Zealand Herald,* the country's largest circulation daily newspaper, had to say of my win:

"There has never been a performance like Charles' in New Zealand golf; the young bank clerk showed that he had the game, the mental approach and a maturity of concentration not usually associated with one so youthful, especially in a sport so fiercely competitive as big time golf. . . ."

With that title, I was suddenly in demand for exhibitions. It was after one such appearance in the company of South African A. D. (Bobby) Locke, winner of the British Open three times by that stage (he won again in 1957), that he said this of my game to the media:

"I like him as a golfer very much. I like the way he steps up and hits the ball. I like the way he putts — his is a good one . . . I do not consider that Charles' development will be restricted because he is a left-hander. That, in golf, is a common fallacy. I don't agree with the argument that because a man is a left-hander he cannot reach the heights."

During those early years I learned my game from my parents. It was not until I moved to Christchurch when I was twenty that I had my first lesson from a true golf professional — and New Zealand's best at the time. Mr Harry Blair, resident professional at Christchurch Golf Club, took me under his wing and my game improved a great deal under his watchful and experienced eye.

A golf holiday in the United States and Britain in 1958 was a great education. I played in several major events, including the famed U.S. Masters — for which I had received an invitation on the basis of my amateur achievements. It proved as tough as I had been led to believe, but it was good experience.

I also had the opportunity to watch such fine golfers as Sam Snead, Ben Hogan, Byron Nelson and Cary Middlecoff. They were great to watch and I feel I learned something from just observing them playing.

From the United States we went to Britain where the highlight for me was a place in the 1958 British Open field and also reaching the quarter finals of the British Amateur.

Not long after I got back from that tour I went away again, this time a member of the New Zealand team playing in St Andrews, Scotland, in the World Amateur Teams' Championship for the Eisenhower Trophy. We missed the trophy but I was able to develop my putting to the degree that Pat Ward-Thomas, one of the world's leading golf writers, wrote: "Charles is one of the finest putters in the world."

Late in 1960, I was at Merion in the United States for the second Eisenhower Trophy tournament, my presence as one of the only two left-handers in the World Championship arousing considerable attention.

Another media comment, this time from the Philadelphia *Evening Bulletin:* "The fact that he is a left-hander is enough to give him a touch of distinction in the fairway classic. No less an authority than the London *Times* rated him the finest left-handed golfer in the world."

They were certainly writing about me.

With good play at Merion, where I was fourth-best in the individual aggregates, it was time for a decision: whether to turn professional.

I faced the prospect of a transfer by my bank from Christchurch to another city. I didn't want the move. Banking had been good to me but I took the plunge and within a few weeks was on an airliner bound for tournaments in South Africa.

In my pocket I had a round-the-world air ticket and a few hundred dollars. This was not a trip to gain experience . . . it was the real thing.

If I failed, and if I spent the dollars I had, I knew I would have to catch the first plane back home.

But I did not fail. Nine months later I was home again from South Africa and Britain with my pockets full of money. I had also met my wife Verity, who had introduced me to George and Brenda Blumberg, familiar faces around the world golfing circuit.

South African professional Gary Player.

Through George I eventually met Mark McCormack, who handled the affairs of Gary Player, Arnold Palmer, Jack Nicklaus and Doug Sanders. Mark agreed to represent me also. Our only contract is still what it has always been: a handshake. It has meant a tremendous amount having Mark represent me.

After a couple of tournaments in South Africa early in 1963, Verity and I left for the United States and the 1963 PGA tour — my first full programme on the American circuit. The highlight was Houston, where I hit the top.

With final rounds of 66 and 69 for a record four-round total of 268 I won the tournament by one stroke from a fast-finishing Fred Hawkins. And shortly after I was standing holding a cheque for $10,000 — it was hard to believe, a great thrill.

The media dined out on my Houston victory, sports pages across the country heaping me with columns of praise. It was a major victory which helped confirm that I had made the right decision in turning professional. I was pleased to have made my mark on the game in a relatively short

With Ben Hogan at the famous Augusta National Golf Club, Georgia, U.S.A. *Bill Mark*

time and at a period when competition was exceptionally fierce as scores of fine players sought to establish reputations and bank balances.

Clearly, what I had learned about golf from babyhood through into manhood proved to be the right "mix" for the Houston and British Open victories of 1963. From there I moved into the top flight of world professional golf, establishing myself through the late 1960s, on into the 70s and now in the 80s as a golfer able to meet — and sometimes beat — the best, despite my standing on the "other side of the ball"

I still show some of the form of bygone days — even though I now wear glasses. After a long lay-off over the summer of 1983-4, I returned to the British and European tours where, after a disappointing start, I recorded good finishes in the West German, Swiss and European Open championships. It was the German event in Frankfurt where the benefit of glasses first made itself felt, and I finished in third place after leading the field going into the final round. I came in the top ten in the two other European finishes — those glasses were certainly working.

Both on and off the golf course I feel at ease with people, even though at one stage I was criticised in New Zealand for what was seen as my lack of emotion and colour.

That is not true and never has been. When I am on the golf course I am out there working, doing a job the best way I know how, just like any other person in any other kind of job. For me, dedication, concentration and the ability to isolate myself from outside distractions are vital when on the job. Of course I acknowledge the applause, and I have always had a good relationship with the media, who have treated me well. I also enjoy the company of other players and

Still on form — with the aid of glasses!

friends at the end of the day's play.

I see myself as an everyday sort of guy who also happens to be the luckiest left-handed golfer in the world.

One of the biggest strokes of luck has been the land of my birth. For its population, there are more left-handed golfers in New Zealand than anywhere else in the world. I was not discouraged by others for being left-handed and no-one tried to change me, because I was not seen as an oddity. I was among many left-handers.

I have also been lucky with my parents: first because they encouraged and helped me so much, and second because they were also left-handers.

I may not have won as many events as Jack Nicklaus, Arnold Palmer or Gary Player, but I feel I have left an imprint on the game of golf, and I look forward to the future as a senior with a feeling, not of regret, but of excitement and anticipation. The last 25 years as a professional golfer have certainly been rewarding. I have enjoyed them as I intend to enjoy the future.

The Charles stance and tee line-up — playing in the New Zealand Open 1976, then sponsored by BP (NZ) Ltd.

Chapter One

Technique, attitude and preparation

SUCCESS in any sphere of life, whether it be business or sport, is something we all seek, but don't always find. Golfers, amateur or professional, are no different from anyone else.

Statistics show that no golfer ever achieves 100 per cent success in competition. To attain such a goal would require a perfect game and also a never-ending run of luck. But there is no reason why the golfer shouldn't always have his or her sights set on perfection at every outing.

In my long career in the highly competitive arena of amateur and professional golf, I have sought perfection from the time of hitting my first warm-up shot until sinking the last putt of the day.

Setting me on the right course has been a sound swing which I was fortunate to develop at an early age, thanks to my parents who as keen and determined players themselves, understood the workings of the golf swing and passed their thoughts and ideas on to me. We are all left-handers, so the learning process was straightforward. I also spent considerable time studying photographs from golf books by Ben Hogan and Sam Snead. In my view hitting a golf ball correctly is quite simple although many people get themselves into all sorts of peculiar and often ungainly attitudes to make sure the ball moves forward.

In my earlier book, *Left-Handed Golf* published in 1965, I said that everyone who plays golf is going to have some days that are much better than others; I've no reason to change my opinion some 20 years on. There are days when timing is bad and your game falls to pieces no matter how hard you try to correct yourself. Fortunately, bad days enable those of us with sound swings to put those "black" periods behind us, knowing the next day's play will be better.

Simplicity is the basis of a sound swing. As a young man, about the time I won the New Zealand Open title as an amateur in 1954, I hit the ball with considerable accuracy off the tee. My middle to short game was sound and the early confidence I established on the putting green due to hundreds of hours of practice gave me a generally sound game overall. I was capable of playing par or better in good conditions, but was still open to improvement.

When I turned professional in late 1960, my long game was short by accepted international standards for touring players, but with constant play week after week on the world circuits, I gradually increased my length between 1963 and 1965, until I was hitting the ball perhaps a little longer than the average professional. I also acquired a slight draw which helped to increase my length.

In 1966, my draw turned to a wild, uncontrollable hook. Something had to be done so I took a lesson late in the year from top United States teacher Bob Toski, who said my problem was one of grip: I was gripping the club far too tightly. On Toski's advice, I developed a fade almost from the moment I started putting into practice what he told me. This fade gave me more control of shot.

My friend Volker Krajewski.

In later years, I found myself experiencing further problems and was fortunate to be in the right place at the right time to do something about it. One of these places was Scotland, the time was 1982 during the British Open. My play from the tee was erratic and as I turned myself inside out on the practice tee after a poor opening round, I caught sight of an old friend, Volker Krajewski, whom I had met years earlier on the United States tour. His lifestyle had changed; the prestigious position of resident professional at the Geneva Golf Club in Switzerland was his new found calling.

Volker Krajewski took a look at me and soon diagnosed the problem. I was, as Bob Toski had observed years earlier, gripping the club far too tightly. I worked at relaxing my grip, with results that soon had me hitting the ball enormous distances for me. Suddenly I was at home with my game once again.

Are lefties different?

Left-handers or lefties play the same game as right-handers. Born a natural left-hander at golf, I have, as you would expect, developed my total game on the "other" side of the ball with what I feel have been generally satisfactory results. In my long experience as a professional I have not found the strategy of play any different, the physical approach any better or worse, or the mechanics of the swing any harder to master.

Occasionally, the fact that I am a left-hander on a certain hole can provide problems. One of these is the 13th at Augusta National, home of the famed Masters, which is a par five dog-leg to the left that can be reached in two if the drive is long and correctly placed.

This particular hole is made to order for the right-hander who can draw or hook his tee shot into position. For me, however, a right to left movement of the ball could cost, not add, distance. This is because a ball that fades has neither the distance nor the added roll that a controlled draw or hook has.

On balance, I think that of the hundreds of courses I have played during my career, there has been nothing in their design and construction which has disadvantaged me because I'm a leftie. The Augusta dog-leg and perhaps one or two others are rare exceptions. I disagree with the argument that left-handed golfers are penalised by course design. There are dog-legs going to the left; equally there are dog-legs going to the right. There are also out of bounds to the left and to the right. There are trees to the right, and to the left.

If, however, all the trees, bunkers and dog-legs were on the one side, then I would have to agree that courses were designed and built for a certain kind of player.

In professional golf, the pin placements are selected daily with no favouritism for one player over another. There are generally six pin placements to the *right*; six to the *left*; and six in the *centre*. This variation in the pin placement gives scope for a left-hander among tournament fields of predominantly right-handers.

I feel it is worth mentioning that the design of the Royal Lytham and St Annes links where I won the British Open in 1963 has out of bounds on the right of almost every hole. This is perhaps an advantage for a left-hander in that he is facing away from the trouble. In New Zealand, the Titirangi course where I won the 1978 Air New Zealand Shell Open has much of the trouble on the right of the fairway, at my back. And the famous St Andrews course in Scotland is another with much of the trouble on the right side of the fairway. So on these courses the left-hander has an advantage.

The Rules of Golf for lefties are the same, course manners are the same and scoring is the same. I've heard it said that I'm some sort of guru and unique in this Royal and Ancient game. Not so. I'm a natural leftie at golf, baseball and cricket, but I'm right-handed when using one hand and left-handed with two. That is, I extend the left hand below the right when *two* are required. But when using one hand, I am right-handed.

In fact, I am basically right-handed, right-eyed, and right-footed which I think is perhaps an advantage because I am always looking to my right using my strong right eye.

As a left-handed golfer, I've been able to tune my game to bring me titles and a way of life which though demanding has enabled me to follow a satisfying career and enjoy a comfortable lifestyle. I wouldn't swap it for that first job I had as a bank clerk even though I was then counting money every day!

Value of lessons

Teaching golf is certainly an interesting profession, but it is no bed of roses. It is often frustrating, sometimes drab, maybe even painful and in some countries it is not as financially rewarding as it might at first appear.

Fortunately there are times when a particular pupil will apply him or herself to getting right the lessons the professional has passed on, and will work at the game, finally going on to win tournaments. There are no fast roads to success in this Royal and Ancient game; hard work and application are the only paths to rewards.

From time to time a teaching professional will be faced with a unique problem. It usually goes something like this:

A player of promise walks into the professional's shop and says, "I've been playing the game for years. I've been scoring well, but feel I can do better. But don't change my swing. Just get rid of my slice and don't waste my time."

To keep the client happy the pro will have to give the impatient golfer a quick remedy which will certainly cure the slice, but which is likely to add a hook to the client's shots.

This is an exaggerated example, but it shows what can happen if a golfer does not begin well by going to a pro as he or she develops competence at the game and getting advice about eliminating faults before settling into a groove which gives reasonable scores, but in the wrong way.

If you are determined to do well at the game, get yourself to a teaching professional as quickly as possible. Talk about your aims and aspirations and be prepared to devote hours to putting into practice what you have been taught. Don't be afraid to open up to the pro with your ideas and any problems which restrict your movement. Many would-be golfers are too shy to ask for lessons. This is unfortunate because they are by-passing an almost guaranteed short-cut to enjoyable golf. When someone boasts of never having taken a lesson, that person is more to be pitied than envied.

If you have a physical disability, tell your pro. Most teachers will be able to guide you into developing an efficient swing around any such problem. Listen carefully but avoid nodding yes to everything unless you understand completely. Often, advice that is perfectly clear on the practice tee gets jumbled up when you go out on the course, and instead of your game improving, it gets worse. The value of communication can never be overestimated. Once you and the teacher are on the same wavelength the instruction becomes permanent. Then whenever your game sours, it is relatively easy to find the error on the practice tee.

Attempting to correct a fault by yourself is foolhardy. Even the touring professionals are not always able to diagnose their own games to this extent.

When lesson time is up, do not rush out to the course to try to put the instructor's tips into immediate use. Try to practise everything that was covered until you make the new skills a part of your game that you can rely on. Haste in trying to beat hell out of the ball using your professional's advice, before warming up adequately, is likely to result in your time as well as your teacher's being wasted. Patience is essential.

Golf lessons are not confined to professionals passing on the benefits of their experience and training to amateurs. Tournament professionals are not perfectionists at all times. Golf would be a very dull game indeed if that were so. No one, regardless of handicap, is beyond asking for a session with a teaching professional, if only to have a competent person watching his or her swing. A major tournament rarely goes by without one hearing of one pro giving another, usually an opponent, a tip to correct some fault.

If the pros themselves need this type of scrutiny, weekend players must need it also. An investment in a good teaching professional will almost certainly give you a good return.

Practice

To ask the majority of amateurs to practise before they play is expecting too much. But this is more because of the game's attractiveness than a criticism of the players. They might have the extra free time, but there are also activities other than golf, so it isn't surprising that the average player prefers to get up and go rather than warm up adequately. If you can't find time to warm up before teeing off, try to do some limbering up exercises in the locker room, or exercise your fingers and arms to make sure they at least are relaxed.

Take to the practice area some particular problem you want to work on, and stay with it until you have it resolved to your satisfaction. If you cannot solve your problem alone, get the assistance of your professional. Do not ask advice of a friend, a bystander or anyone else. This can do harm.

Do not go to the practice area just to hit golf balls. Follow a plan and aim for a target. As a warm up for a tournament or a friendly round, start with the short irons and work up through the middle and long irons, then the woods to the driver; then try to fit in a session with the wedge approach shots and some putting. Do not overdo it if you are scheduled for an early tee off.

Never practise when you are tired, or the session will only add to the problems. Take plenty of time between hits, and stay relaxed. Spend a lot of time on "type" shots, that is, the deliberate hook, slice, low or high ball.

Experiment and improve; learn to play the wind shots; try hitting balls from tight lies with every club in the bag; discover the many uses of the wedge; learn how to hit them high or low with this valuable club and when possible, practise those hilly lies.

The practice area is golf's incubator. There, questions about the mechanics of the game are answered, experiments are proved and disproved, swings are grooved, and confidence restored.

Exercise

The first practice hint is to spend a few minutes daily to just grip and re-grip a golf club, to get accustomed to the right grip and also to retain the feel for the club. This is especially beneficial to the high handicap golfer. Take the grip in your right hand and then in your left, then get both hands correctly on the grip, and give the club a little wiggle. You do not need a full swing; merely by gripping and re-gripping, getting a feel of the club for these few minutes daily, you will strengthen your hand muscles and keep your hands, fingers, wrists and forearms in the right groove, ready for action on the weekend.

The second hint is to swing a weighted club or, if one isn't available, use one of those weighted head covers that can slip over the head of your regular club. It is an excellent warm-up device, one that will slow your swing down a lot. You will soon develop rhythm as well as a slow, easy, efficient swing. You will strengthen not only your wrists, but all your golfing muscles. Swinging a weighted club stretches the muscles, and stretching helps you to turn in the backswing. This will help you get the necessary extra distance.

The *mirror* can also help you. A full length mirror can help you check on any movement of the head. I suggest a steady head position throughout, because I believe that the head, next to the hands, is one of the foundations of a good swing. I like to see it remain in the same position from the time the club is started back until after you've hit the ball. Try to keep your head steady. It should remain fixed and you should swing around it. Imagine your head nailed to something behind you and swing around it.

Looking in the mirror will also give you an idea of whether you are actually gripping the club correctly, whether the grip you are using is holding the club in the correct plane. It can point out any swaying movement, any incorrect roll of the wrist, and whether you are lining up to the shot correctly. I see the mirror as one very important aid in getting to know a little bit more about the game and the way you play it.

I'm also a great advocate of physical exercises, but I caution against developing muscles not used in a good golf game. For instance, swimming is not really a good exercise for golf, although swimming is one of the greatest activities for exercising just about every muscle in the body. I prefer golf isometrics, devices that strengthen the wrists, hands and fingers, and anything you can do to keep the legs in shape and your body in top physical condition.

All these exercises will build up the proper golfing muscles and improve your golf, though it is important that you never do any exercise to excess.

Lefties' Equipment

Major developments in golf equipment over the past 20 years have benefited all who play the game, including those of us who stand on the "other side of the ball". Today you can buy a set of perfectly matched equipment — clubs in a particular set that belong to each other in feel, swing-weight and balance.

Your club professional or local retail sports store with trained staff should be able to advise you on all aspects of selection to make sure you get the clubs that are right for you.

Club making is a scientific art and as a left-hander who plays the game for a living, I count myself fortunate to have a good selection of equipment.

Although the range of clubs available is large, not everyone is satisfied with modern developments. Occasionally a golfer may be forced into using a strange set of clubs and he may play his best round of the year with them, or he may purchase an expensive new set that has everything but the feel of the faithful old set hanging in the garage.

Experience and results have shown that

you will perform in accordance with your tools, provided they *fit* you. The finest clubs in the world will do no good for you or your game if they are of the wrong length or lie, or have the wrong shaft for your swing. Any grip that doesn't suit your hands and affects your feel can also cause problems.

Suitable clubs are available. Be selective and use expert advice.

I shudder when I remember how few selections were available to left-handers when I started out in the game. In some areas there were no left-handed clubs at all, and the enthusiast had to hit them from the wrong side if he or she wanted to play golf.

Although individual shapes and sizes vary, most of our arms are approximately the same distance from the ground, the factor in determining correct club length. Most of the standard sets of clubs fall within this length. Manufacturers have succeeded in standardising the balance and feel in each of the three most common shaft deflections — *Stiff*, *Medium* and *Flexible*, so a purchaser can generally be assured that the clubs selected will deliver to the maximum of the player's skills. It's a great time for club buyers, especially left-handers who were for so long a neglected minority.

High in the advancement of today's irons is the feel each club has, the result of pre-determining shaft and head weights to produce a club to a given and desirable swing weight.

Swing weight is an arbitrary measurement indicating the distribution of the weight of the club. It is the ratio of the weight in the head to the shaft and the grip, and is measured on a logarithm scale. The higher the swing weight, the heavier the club will feel. Swing weight should not be confused with total weight, which is actual weight and will vary among clubs within the same set, especially the irons which get heavier in actual weight as they go up in number. Swing weight gives the club its balance. This can be changed if you build up the grips by yourself or if you try to repair the club with tape or if you lengthen or shorten the shaft, and it can be spotted quite easily by those who golf regularly.

It is important to get the right shaft for you. It is usually not too difficult to select the correct shaft from among the stiff, medium and flexible range. Your strength, muscle tone, age, golf ability and swing habits should be considered in your selection. A person who swings easily might find that the flexible shaft provides just the right amount of extra help needed to get extra distance with his or her present swing. The strong hitter would find this club too flexible and too uncontrollable and would be better using a stiff shaft. The medium, of course, will be for the medium person.

It is not too difficult to tell if the shaft you are using is too stiff: in time you'll find that your arms will begin to tire just above the wrists, you will lose the use of the wrists, and the club will feel heavy and unbending. Then it will be time to switch to a shaft with the medium flex. You will know if the shaft is too flexible by a lack of control and clubhead feel.

Remember that the distance your hands are from the ground determines the length of the shaft for you. Let your arms hang down naturally as you stand fairly normally, in just a slight crouch. Grip the club you are thinking of buying and assume your address position, then look at the sole of the club. Better yet, have a competent person check it for you. If it is fairly flat to the ground, with the toe just slightly up, say about ⅛ in. (3 mm), then it would have the proper lie for you. (The lie is the angle measured from the bottom of the club back to the shaft.) The most carefully matched, finest balanced, most expensive set of clubs in the world will be of little value if the lie is not right for you.

Extra long clubs are available, sometimes in open stock, but always on special order. Mine are ¾ in. (19 mm) longer than standard. Some golfers use drivers that are much longer than standard to generate more clubhead speed at impact and thus get more distance. This is valid, but if the longer driver can't be handled, it won't do what it is supposed to, and you will sacrifice not only accuracy but money as well.

The majority of golfers can get along fine with medium shafts, a D1 to D4 swing weight, the prescribed lofts standardised by the manufacturers, and the standard size grip. But since all balance and feel of the club is transmitted through the hands, the proper grip for you is important. You can select from leather, rubber, composition and all-weather types. I suggest you try them all, and decide for yourself.

Grip size is extremely important, because one that is too small will force you into gripping the club too tightly, taking away feel, rhythm and control, while one that is too large will lighten the head and tend to induce an improper swing. Grip size is usually measured at a point 2 in. (5 cm) from the top. Because I have long fingers and because I was inclined to grip tightly, my grips are larger than normal.

The key to good golf is the club you are using, and today's golf club is a superbly tailored instrument. I am not suggesting you throw away your old clubs and run out to buy a new set, but amateurs very often hang onto clubs that should have been retired. Their reasons include financial difficulties, which is all right, of course; preference for the old over the new will be tough to prove and very simple to disprove; or superstition, they won a big championship with them. All of this is understandable but foolhardy, if the golfer has ambitions of improving his pleasure.

Today's clubs are the finest. If you use them, you will play your finest too.

Caring for your golf gear

Walk into the club storeroom of many golf courses and the chances are that you will find your resident professional and his staff have cleaned all the clubs and made them ready for the next round. But club storage takes care of only a few. Most players keep their own clubs.

Gripping a right-handed club. With me are Bob Goalby (left) and Gene Sarazen, a legend in world professional golf. The occasion was the Shell Wonderful World of Golf Series in New Zealand, 1968.

Far too many golfers fail to look after their clubs. Equipment is thrown into the boot of the car at the end of one day's play and pulled out a week or so later for the next round, still carrying dirt.

Gear that is well looked after will last; it will also give you a feeling of confidence when you step onto the first tee.

On the other hand, gear which is allowed to gather dirt week after week must deteriorate and also have a detrimental effect on one's game.

Keep your gear in good order and your golf will reflect the pride you take in it.

Today many newcomers to golf start with just a few clubs — I did, and so did thousands of others before having enough money to buy a set of matched woods and irons, a bag, a trolley and other important accessories such as shoes, wet weather gear, and, of course, a good supply of golf balls.

Since I became a professional more than 20 years ago, there has been a revolution in the development of equipment, especially clubs. No new club appears on the shelves of a sports store or in your club professional's shop without having been subjected to a most thorough planning programme involving designers, engineers, toolmakers and often consultant professionals.

But, it is the end user, the golfer, who has the final say about what equipment he or she wants. The user will also decide how the equipment should be looked after.

Most golf courses are maintained to a very high standard by using chemical fertilisers. These chemicals can cause rust or pitting in the metal of shafts and clubheads. If left without attention, even for a short time, deterioration will occur and eventually affect the weight and balance of the clubs.

Your new woods will have a high lustre finish, while most brands of irons will have a gleaming polish. With care, it is possible to keep them close to that condition throughout their life.

To keep clubs in good condition apply a coat of furniture polish or one of the many high gloss polishes now available from your golf professional or at any sports or general store. Most of these polishes will also remove marks or grass stains.

Keep the woods protected with head covers, or they will rub against each other in the bag, causing scratches that may ruin them. If the head covers get wet, remove them as soon as you complete the round. Dry them thoroughly before re-using them.

If your wood club is reinforced with neck whipping, keep it intact. If this thread breaks, have your club re-wound with thread. Do not use tape in a do-it-yourself attempt to repair. Even an additional ⅛ ounce to the clubhead can change the swing weight of the club.

Today's woods are stronger and better looking than those of years past, but they must be given some care if you expect them to play and look their best.

The irons, too, have undergone many changes and improvements over the past 20 years, but the reasons for keeping them clean are unchanged. You can't play your best with equipment that is clogged with mud or dried grass. Not only will the balance be affected, but the ball will react abnormally when hit. You will control the shot much better when you keep the clubface free of dirt.

All that is needed, at the end of the round, is a soaking in soap and water followed by a rinse and a wipe. Do not use harsh brushes, steel wool or abrasives, or you will cut through the nickel-chrome plating, ruining the club's appearance and balance.

During play you can scrape very gently any clogging in the face scoring (lines) with the pointed end of a tee, or you could use a wet towel.

The top end of the club must also be considered. The grips are noticeably improved, but through constant use or abuse, they may become frayed or worn. Resist the impulse to save money by building them up with tape. The addition of 1/32 in. (0.75 mm) to the grip reduces the swing weight by at least one point.

The shafts have to be taken care of too. Be careful how you pack your clubs in your car. It does them no good if they are packed into the boot under heavy luggage. And don't bang your clubs into the ground in disgust. This treatment will bend the shafts and ruin the clubs' balance and precision.

Footwear and bags

Give some care to your golf shoes. They carry most of the weight, so make certain they fit and feel as comfortable at the end of the round as they did at the outset. Treat them with a good leather conditioner and use shoetrees to maintain their shape. Remove grass and dirt from the spikes and soles before placing them in your locker, carry-all bag or car boot. The spikes are functional; they help you keep your balance while executing the shot. Check periodically for any that might be loose or missing. I suggest you have at least two good pairs of shoes.

Your golf bag must be plenty big enough to contain the number of clubs you find necessary to use. Too often a small bag is purchased and the golfer then has to jam the full complement of clubs into too small a space, raising havoc with the grips and endangering the shafts. If your bag is leather, treat it regularly with the good leather conditioner you have used on your golf shoes. This will prevent cracking and will protect against excessive wear while adding to its looks.

Replace the strap when there is evidence of wear, and avoid the inconvenience of a possible strap break in the middle of a round. Also check the condition of the pockets and zips and avoid the expense of losing costly items you have stored inside the pockets. Do not allow anyone to sit on the bag. This will destroy the rings that give it its shape and strength.

Though the initial cost of top grade golf equipment is high, a little care will make the investment last a lifetime. When you buy the best and protect it, you play better, get more for your money, look better, enjoy the game to the fullest and maybe even win a few trophies!

My clubs

No matter where I play, people want to know about my clubs. Indeed, on the practice tee or on the course you will see people looking at the equipment carried by professionals.

Details of my clubs are:

Woods

Driver: A Precision X shaft which is in the flexible range of X classifications.

3 and 4 Woods: Pro-fit Stiff Shaft.

Irons

All have Dynamic (S) Stiff Shafts.

CLUBS

Woods	**Swing**	**Deadweight Ozs.**	**(Grams)**
driver	D2.5	13.40 ozs	(379.9 g)
3 wood	D2.5	13.55 ozs	(384.2 g)
4 wood	D2.5	13.60 ozs	(385.6 g)
Irons			
No. 2	D1.00	14.80 ozs	(419.5 g)
3	D1.00	15.00 ozs	(425.2 g)
4	D1.50	15.20 ozs	(430.8 g)
5	D1.50	15.40 ozs	(436.5 g)
6	D3.00	15.70 ozs	(445.0 g)
7	D3.00	15.95 ozs	(449.2 g)
8	D4.00	16.25 ozs	(461.5 g)
9	D5.50	16.45 ozs	(467.1 g)
Wedge	D6.00	16.95 ozs	(480.5 g)
Sand wedge	D6.00	16.75 ozs	(474.8 g)
Putter	D5.50	17.85 ozs	(506.0 g)

Preparation for play

Physical and mental preparation complement each other in any sport, and golf is no exception.

My association with longtime friend Gary Player has helped me to understand the importance of physical fitness for one's wellbeing, and though we have never discussed the mental aspect of the game at any length, we have often talked of the need for good health and a fairly disciplined lifestyle if personal goals are to be attained.

Back in the early 1970s Gary introduced me to jogging which I pursued for some time, mainly on beaches or around golf courses rather than through city traffic as appears to be the practice of many athletes these days.

I no longer jog, although the miles I put in during the early 1970s were a factor in my excellent results from a stress test on a treadmill at the Dallas Aerobic Clinic in 1978. On a return visit to the Clinic about three years later, my treadmill tests showed an improvement on my earlier examination, confirming my belief in a limited jogging programme coupled with attention to diet.

Because of my touring programme, I now spend several months each summer on my farm in New Zealand, and the physical work there is another contributing factor to my good physical condition. Indeed, physically, I feel better than I did 20 years ago. As a result of attention to nutrition — reduction in sugars, salts and fats and an increased intake of fibres — I face the future in the knowledge that body and mind are fine tuned to enable me to prolong my career by several years.

Looking ahead, my intention is to score to the best of my ability, for the Seniors' tour is something I could not have envisaged even five years ago; it didn't exist and by the age of 50 I would under other circumstances probably be playing fewer events than ever before.

Because of my fitness, I can still play all the clubs in my bag with a high degree of proficiency.

Chapter Two

The grip

AS a tall, lean person, I have long, thin fingers, hence my *long thumb grip* which over the years has been commented on by opponents, partners and commentators on the game.

It is true that my grip is a bit unusual.

Firstly, my right hand. I more or less shake hands with the club, gripping it so I can see between two and three knuckles of the right hand, but the right thumb is extended down the grip or top of the shaft in what is called the long thumb (Photograph B).

I feel this gives me more control over the club, especially nearer the top of the swing where it is important. It shortens my backswing and this, of course, is desirable in setting up the downswing the way I like to play it. Being a reasonably tall man — I stand 6 ft 1½ in. (1.85 m) and thin — I'm inclined to stand closer to the ball than a shorter person would. I therefore have a fairly upright swing and my long thumb helps keep the club in the right *arc* for me.

At the takeaway I extend straight back from the ball in my fairly upright three-quarter swing. I also have a high follow through, and stress the importance of keeping the plane of the swing on the same *arc* in the backswing as in the downswing. My grip enables me to use this swing the way I want to for what I feel are the best results for me.

It has been said and written about many times that no two grips are alike and I cannot disagree with that.

When gripping the club with the long thumb, there is a less noticeable V between the thumb and the index finger of the right hand than that ordinarily formed by the advocates of the short thumb method.

A A close-up of my grip.

The short thumb might be the correct grip for you, and if you find this is so and you employ it, keep the V of both the right and left hands aligned and pointing upwards toward the chin or left shoulder. However, with the short thumb, I feel that the golfer will be holding the club more in the fingers, which can experience a change in feel from day to day. With so much more room for error, there would be more difficulty in controlling the clubhead. One of the golfer's most common faults is losing control of the clubhead at the top of the swing, and one of the causes is the piccolo grip that is loose at the top, with a fingers-only grip. If the club is held more in the palm of the right hand and in the fingers of the left, the grip will stay firm all the way through.

With the right hand shaking hands with the club, place the left on the club so the pocket formed between the left thumb and the palm fits on top of the right thumb (Photograph C). The back of the left hand is now facing away from the target, and both hands are positioned to form the V between the thumb and forefinger. The left hand V is pointing towards the left shoulder, and the right hand V is pointing towards the chin.

I use the Vardon grip which is favoured by most of the golfers I've competed against. It is also known as the overlapping grip because the little finger of the left supposedly overlaps the forefinger of the right. Actually, however, my left little finger is hooked between the index finger and the middle finger of the right. This is a minor variation and is entirely up to personal adjustment and feel.

Technically, grips are rather like fingerprints, none is exactly like anyone else's.

If your fingers are short, I suggest the interlocking grip. Position the hands as described above, but interlock the little finger of the left hand with the forefinger of the right.

Those with weak hands might be better using the full-fingered grip or double-handed grip which spreads the hands more on the grip of the club.

During my long career, I have used all three grips with varying degrees of success.

Initially, I used the double-handed grip, with all fingers of both hands on the club and the right hand thumb on the shaft. This was satisfactory until I was about 12 years old when I developed and used the interlocking grip, not only because I had small hands and short fingers at the time, but also, I suppose, because my father who was a very good golfer used it most successfully. I changed to my present overlapping grip at the age of 18 just before winning the 1954 New Zealand Open.

B The grip: the right hand is on the shaft with the thumb straight down the grip of the club. The club is gripped more in the palm of the right hand, with the fingers close together.

Over the years, I have made few changes to my grip. From time to time, I move both hands a fraction to rectify a problem. If I keep fading the ball or if I'm too strong and hooking, I compensate by moving my hands slightly into a weaker position for hooking or a stronger position for fading. These are the only changes I make with my grip, a policy I have followed right through

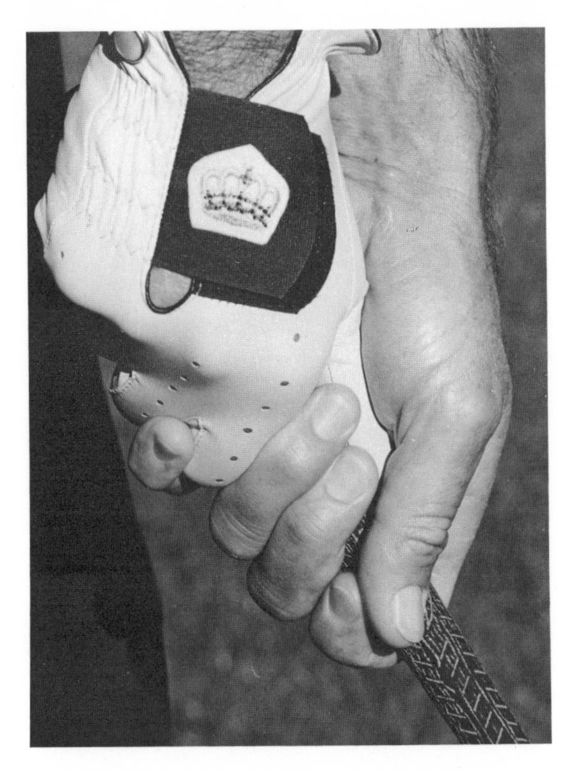

C Front view of the overlap grip: when viewed by the golfer, three to four knuckles of the right hand will be seen. The club is in the fingers of the left hand, the fingers are close together and the thumb is in a pocket formed by the palm and thumb of the left hand. The little finger of the left hand overlaps the first two fingers of the right hand — in the groove between them.

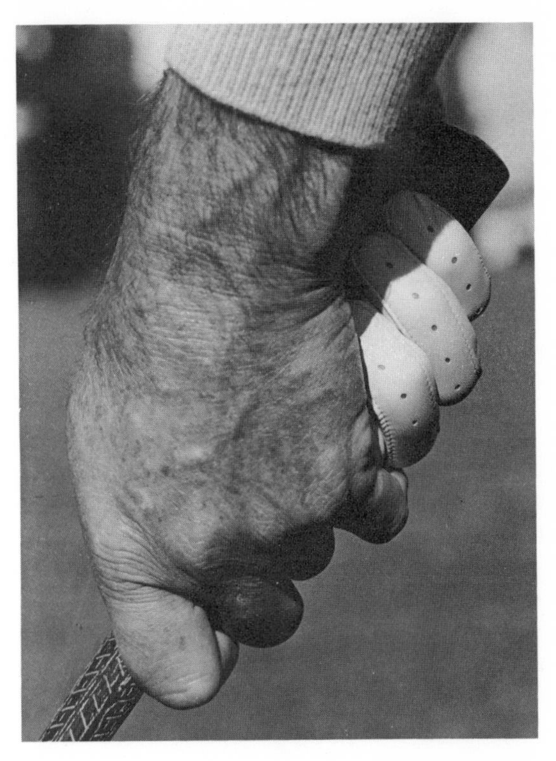

D Rear view of the overlap grip showing fingers close together on the club with the little finger overlapping. This is a good example of the back of the left hand facing directly away from the target.

my career. In essence they are only remedial changes.

It is important to have the fingers of both hands as close together as possible. I have noticed that many amateurs spread the index finger of the left hand down the shaft. This, I believe, decreases the feel between thumb and forefinger and also decreases the leverage in the swing. Correct hand action is necessary for maximum distance.

I have also seen many players, most of them amateurs, gripping the club very hard in the belief that a very tight grip will enable them to give the ball a harder wallop. This is wrong. The opposite is true: a lighter grip gives more distance.

A tight grip restricts the backswing and the natural *arc* of the club. You should make no conscious effort to grip any more firmly with either hand, as both hands work together as a unit. There should be no tension. A firm, relaxed positioning of both hands on the club will provide an easy, relaxed swing which should enable you to hit the ball well.

When you are standing up to the ball, preparing to start the swing, everything should be in a relaxed, comfortable position. The club will not fall from your hands. Nor are you in any danger of squeezing the life out of it. At the top your hands should be as firm as at address, so you are able to swing freely and hit the ball solidly. Posi-

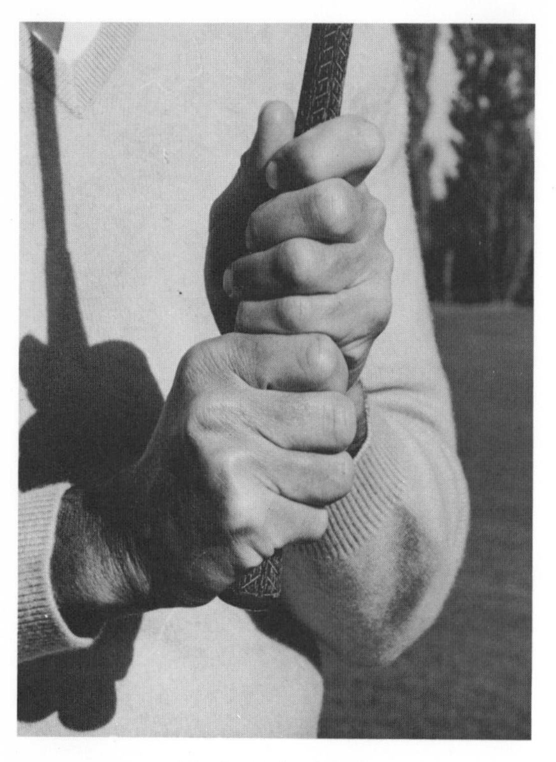

E Double handed grip.

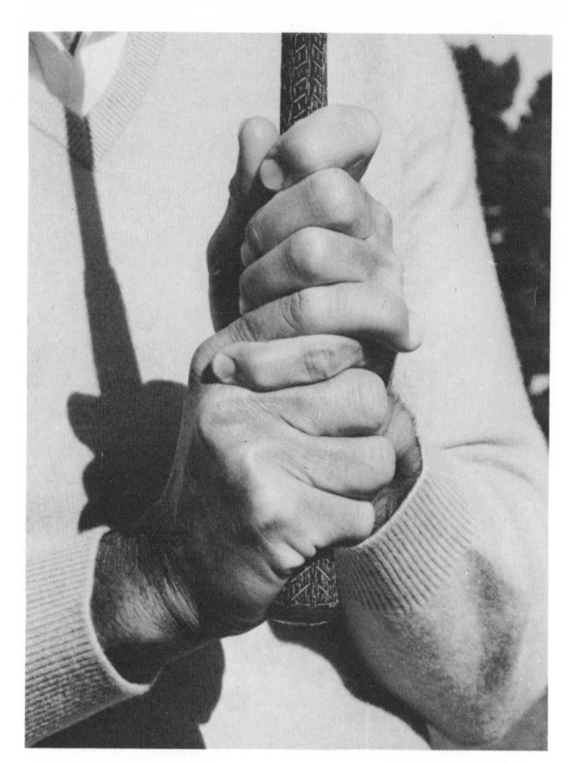

F Interlocking grip.

tioned as you are at the top, with the hands poised to come into the hitting area in the same position they were at address, you will know the ball is going to be on the line of flight you have selected. Transmitting all the power and direction through the body, shoulders, arms and hands into the fingers further emphasises the need for the correct grip, and if it is uncomfortable for you at the beginning, do not despair; more importantly, do not change it to something easier.

Do everything or anything but change the grip and, when you have experienced the feel of both hands guiding the club back and controlling the speed of the swing as well as the direction of the clubhead, you will be well on your way to the best golf you will ever play. There is no other way, if an efficient swing and success are your goals.

Chapter Three

The stance or address

AT address, I believe every part of your anatomy should be in a square position — the feet, knees, hips, shoulder, all should be square and parallel to the line of flight. This stance should be cultivated, practised, rehearsed, until it is almost automatic. It sets up all the subsequent movements, it simplifies the swing, and it prevents other small but damaging faults from creeping into the movement and ruining the shot before it begins.

Alignment procedure should be accorded

I am illustrating my stance with a patented American device, the Funk Setup Master.

A driver front The ball is positioned just off the right heel. The feet are a comfortable distance apart — about the width of the shoulders for the driver. The weight is evenly distributed between the left and right feet, and the hands are positioned in line over the ball — that is with the shaft pointing in a line to the right of the chin.

B driver rear Note that the feet, knees, hips and shoulders are parallel to the line of flight. The knees are relaxed and the back is straight and not hunched or arched. The weight is evenly distributed between the heels and toes, allowing for a comfortable position over the ball. Plenty of room is allowed for the hands to swing the club. The back of the left hand is facing away from the target.

C No. 5 iron front The weight is evenly distributed between the left and right feet. However, the feet are closer together than for the driver, with the ball positioned further back in the stance. The hands are slightly ahead of the ball. Note the angle of the club shaft.

D No. 5 iron rear The stance is still square to the line of flight, with the weight distribution still even between the heels and toes. The ball is now closer to the feet with the hands a comfortable distance from the body.

a special place in any book on golf instruction. No golfer is immune to the careless act of occasionally standing up to a ball incorrectly. This will always cause a bad shot no matter how perfectly the ball is stroked. To avoid this, most golfers make a special ritual about alignment, but since most of it is taking place as the golfer is walking up to the ball, it goes unnoticed.

The safest and surest way to line up the shot is to check the direction from behind the ball. If you do this, your direction is easily and accurately gauged. Once the line has been solved, you should work on setting your feet square to it. Then everything else should fall into place in a regular pattern, with the hips and shoulders lining themselves up automatically.

The photographs show a series of address sequences.

Accomplished, or I should say correct, players probably started their careers by using the square method as the formation and eventual basis of their game. Everything from top to bottom is square with the hole as in Photographs A and B (driver), C and D (mid irons), E and F (wedge). All things being equal, this should result in the clubface at the point of impact being square — essential for straight flight.

Naturally, not everyone will be happy with the square method. There are variations, especially among professionals, some of whom work best from an open stance (Photograph B) or closed stance (Photograph C). Although the professionals will

E wedge front The feet are quite close together for the wedge with the ball positioned towards the centre of the stance. The hands are ahead of the ball, with the weight evenly distributed. As with the driver, note the straight right arm.

F wedge rear The stance is now slightly open with feet, hips and shoulders. The ball is positioned close to the feet but still allows freedom to swing. The grip is the same as for the driver, with the back left hand still facing away from the target.

not always stand square to the line and will look different at address, they are, in fact, alike in the important impact zone, and the club face does come through the ball square to the hole. I use a square stance with the *woods, long irons* and *medium irons,* but with the *shorter irons* and *wedges* I tend to open my stance fractionally because I find this more comfortable and it gives me a shorter swing plane with more control.

Photograph A illustrates the square position of the feet, knees, hips and shoulders. A line drawn between the feet would parallel the line of flight. An open stance would have the same components pointing to the right of the target. Pulling your right foot back from the line would open the stance as in Photograph B. When the left foot is brought back, you are closing your stance, as in Photograph C.

I cannot stress enough the importance of having four parts of the body — feet, knees, hips and shoulders — all parallel with the intended line of flight.

The reason for this square position is that it sets up all the proper subsequent moves. When everything is parallel to the line of flight, the swing is simplified and you can set a pattern for the efficient use of every club in your bag, from driver to putter, from the first move away from the ball, the take-away, body turn, top of the backswing, return to the ball, impact and follow through. The square position is the only way to build a solid foundation to an efficient swing.

The feet are considered to be square

when the line drawn between the toes parallels the line of flight. The knees are flexed, the weight is distributed evenly between the left and the right foot and between the heel and toe, the hips are level, the body is without tension and the head is over the ball. Because there is no tightness, no strain, the chances of your taking the club back smoothly, slowly and in the right track are in your favour, and if the start is correct, the moves that follow will most likely be correct also.

Basic as this step is, it is often the main cause of poorly executed shots. You must align yourself properly before you assume your stance. Beware, also, of unnecessary tension. Poor alignment and too much tension will spoil your shot before you even hit the ball.

The ball position is also important. For the driver the ball should be positioned off the right heel; for fairway woods it should be moved back slightly; move the ball back a little more with each successive club — long irons, middle irons, short irons, until for the wedge the ball will be positioned in the centre of the stance, halfway between the heels of the left and the right foot. The reason for changing this position is the different *arc* of the clubhead for the respective clubs.

The *driver* requires an arc which sweeps the ball off the tee on the upward turn of the arc. The fairway woods are also hit in a sweeping motion at the bottom point of the arc. For the irons, starting with long irons the ball is hit on the downward arc. This means a good shot will disturb the grass under the ball or take a divot. As the ball is moved further back in the stance, a larger divot will be produced. The greater the downward arc and larger the divot, the greater the backspin on the ball. Together with the loft of the club, the backspin gives the ball the correct elevation.

Chapter Four

The swing

ANYONE who plays sport, amateur or professional, has highs and lows and I am no exception. During nearly 25 years as a touring player I have experienced my share of exhilaration and depression — fortunately more of the former than the latter. I have also been lucky to have some experts to help me sort out problems and put me back on the path to success.

Most of my problems have arisen as a result of failings with my swing. Errors have crept in and at times I have had to seek advice to get the ball going long and straight.

Since before 1982 my thoughts and attitudes about the golf swing have changed from those I had in the mid 1960s when I was much younger and enjoying considerable success in the United States, Britain and Europe and in my native New Zealand.

Perhaps one of the less noticeable but important developments in my game has been the *flattening* of my swing. I found my previous upright approach had caused the club to move across the line at the top of the swing. This threw my plane out and caused the downswing to open the clubface at impact. The result: a big push of the ball to the left. This shows how important it is for the club at the top of the swing to be parallel with the intended line of flight. A crossover of position will cause all sorts of problems.

To enable me to consciously flatten my swing I work hard at keeping my right shoulder from dipping under in the backswing; in other words, I turn my shoulders rather than tilt them.

Another feature of my flatter swing is the position of the left elbow which I keep closer into the body throughout the backswing. This gives more control.

The effect of total concentration on a new approach in technique can be quite dramatic. In many of my tournament successes I've gone out with one thought in mind: take the swing. At Greensboro in 1974, I was concentrating on balance and working at keeping my weight more in my heels because I had a bad habit of falling into the shot with weight on the toes. My thoughts when I lined up at Greensboro were to stay on my heels. It worked and I won. Another occasion was the Tallahassee Open of 1983 where I concentrated for 72 holes to perfect a flat plane for my swing. I had cause to smile at the end of that event, for everything fell into place and I became a major tournament winner over four decades.

I can remember three occasions during my professional career when I have received guidance from noted teaching professionals, and I'm pleased I was able to have their services. The first was in 1966 when I was on a real low. I recall that one of the major problems I had was with my tee shots (of course this part of any golfer's game is critical). At that time, I used to draw the ball, moving it a little from left to right. Unfortunately, the draw developed into a rather violent and uncontrollable hook with disastrous consequences. Action was needed and I talked with celebrated American teacher Bob Toski, who felt my problems lay in my grip. I was holding the club with a vice-like grip. I knew I was doing it as I had always had a tendency to grip tightly.

Shortly after my session with Toski, the hook disappeared.

My next occasion for help was 16 years later while playing in the 1982 British Open at Troon. After a disappointing first round of 77, I took myself to the practice tee, more in frustration than anything. There I ran into Volker Krajewski, an old acquaintance from the United States tour, and sought his assistance. Again it was my grip that was causing the problems. "You're squeezing the club on the takeaway. You grip the club too tightly at address," he told me. "Relax your hands to cut down the stress in your swing."

I immediately hit a few shots with his suggestion in mind and quickly noticed an appreciable difference, something I carried through the opening stages of the second round of the Open, going out in 32, a score to boost any player's confidence. Alas, a howling wind on the back nine saw me back in 42 to miss the cut by one shot. But I was swinging better.

Since 1982, I have had another meeting with "V.K." and some good advice. At the Swiss Open at Crans-sur-Sierre in August 1983, "V.K." suggested that I turn my left hip more in the backswing, with a narrower stance.

With my lighter grip on the club and the lengthened backswing, something else has happened to help my game. I now also raise my right heel at the top of the backswing — something I did not do before. The effect of this, together with other attitudes and approaches, add up to a much fuller and lengthy backswing which enables me to add yardage to my shots with no loss of control. You, too, can get improved results.

Taking away the club from the ball is a critical and precise action. Over the years I have noticed that many players, particularly amateurs, take the club away too steeply. A good wrist cock or hand action can only be achieved by extending the club away from the ball in as wide an arc as physically possible. This extension should also continue into the follow through.

When you stand up to the ball, make sure your grip and stance are correct, then as you move into the backswing or takeaway and down through the ball, remember to keep your head still throughout, or at least until after you have hit the ball. Any movement in the head will change the swing plane, and all kinds of faults will develop, generally with serious consequences.

Although it is the *hands* which control the swing it is the *head* with the *eyes* fixed on the ball and the resultant eye-hand co-ordination which decide the outcome of the swing. It is a bit like darts or billiards where the discipline of eyes and hands holds the key to success.

Backswing or takeaway

The swing is the action area of the game.

I always get the feel of the club before actually settling over the ball. Once you have the feel, the all important move away from the ball is triggered by a forward press which is a slight forward movement of the hands or left knee.

But *please* do not squeeze the club and add tension. When starting the backswing or takeaway, it is essential that you move the clubhead, hands and arms in one piece, all at the same time. The shoulders should turn with that one piece movement, ensuring that the clubhead is taken straight back from the ball for an upright plane, or slightly inside the line for a flatter plane.

Many golfers I've played with, especially on those enjoyable pro-am days which are now very much a part of the professional game, seem to find turning with the swing an uncomfortable, even difficult movement. It's not. You don't have to worry about becoming too stiff and freezing in the midst of this action, or swaying, or getting too flat-footed so you take the club too far on that line.

As the shoulders take over, you will quite naturally turn inside the line of flight, then when the hands reach waist height, the wrists start to cock, remaining that way until the top of the backswing is reached, although the actual top will depend on the length of the club you are using and your physique.

I go back no more than three-quarters, but on average, if you were using the longest club in the bag, which is the driver, the top of your swing might be reached when your hands are above your shoulders, and the shaft of the club is horizontal to the ground. As the clubs get shorter, the backswing will be lessened in proportion.

Throughout, the clubface and hands maintain their square position, primarily because there is no rolling of the wrists, or pronating. In golf language, pronation refers to the rolling of the wrists outward and over, resulting in an open clubface at the top of the swing, meaning, of course, that you have to return to the original position by another, but reverse, roll of the wrists coming down. This, I think, is a dangerous, often unreliable movement, especially if the swing is to be kept as simple as possible by reducing the number of steps which make it up. Eliminating this one movement also results in doing away with many other movements that involve every part of the body.

The angle of the arc of the takeaway depends a lot on the build of the person, and every golfer has a different swing plane. The plane is in effect the angle of the arc of your swing. The shorter a golfer is, the flatter he or she will swing. The tall person, like myself, will swing in a more upright plane. Other factors influencing the arc and the clubface position are length of arms and suppleness of wrists, but if you develop clubhead feel and learn to swing without pronation of the wrists, the arms and wrists need not and should not add confusion to what you have to do to hit the golf ball long and straight.

Whether your backswing is flat or as upright as mine, keep it the same in the backswing as on the downswing. A swing that is too much outside the line will lead to a slice, and one that is too much on the inside will produce a hook. If you suddenly realise this is a way to deliberately hook or slice a ball, you are right. But in developing your game, use a straight takeaway and return to the ball in the same plane.

At the top

The top of the backswing is reached when you feel a stiffening of all the muscles in your right shoulder and all down your right side. The right heel may or may not come off the ground. This depends on the club you are using. With the driver and the maximum turn of the hips and shoulders, the heel will possibly lift, so the backswing is not restricted at the top. The weight stays inside the left foot, and your swing has balance. Your weight distribution will favour the left side at this point.

There will be a feeling of pressure making you want to turn your head away from the ball. Resist, if not the actual move itself, at least the tendency to do so. Build your swing around the thought that you are not going to move your head, even though you make a slight movement on the backswing. This is important, and it is vital that you have both eyes fixed on the ball. You must be able to see the ball with both eyes, not just one of them. If you can see it with only one eye, you have turned your swing back too far and your body has turned away from the ball too much. By keeping your head steady and both eyes glued on the ball, you will soon get yourself and your swing under good control.

Your right knee will turn in toward and behind the ball, and your left knee must be slightly flexed, as it was at address. The slight bend in the left knee, often unnoticed, allows you to turn away from the ball smoothly, prevents a breakdown in your swing, and permits you to start the downswing a little easier. If that left knee were to stiffen, a jerking action would develop under the swing, resulting in a loss of rhythm and effectiveness.

At the top of your swing, you'll find that your hips and shoulders are fully turned, that the back of your shoulders will be almost at right angles to the line of flight. You will discover that your chin is tucked into your right shoulder. This provides a second checkpoint: the angle formed by a line running from your shoulders to the ball.

At the top of the swing, your right shoulder must be lower than your left. You will also notice that your hips are at an angle of about 45 degrees, about half that of the shoulders; you should find this position is quite comfortable. I am a great believer in the straight right arm at address and, just as importantly, at the top. I never like to see anyone with a bent right arm, because it means that the arc of the clubhead will be restricted, cutting down the potential of the stroke. So get your right arm quite straight, not exactly poker stiff, but as straight as you can naturally get it. At least, work on getting it to feel as though it is straight.

Another valuable checkpoint is the left elbow. It plays its biggest part in getting your clubhead into the ball properly, but even at this stage its value must be recognised. Tuck it in at address, and visualise how it helps keep the plane of the swing smooth, the clubhead square. Try moving it in different positions and at varying distances from your body. It will be well worth experimenting. After you have experienced the feeling of the elbow brushing in close, or the folly of trying to pack it in too much, or much worse, feeling it fly out away from your body, you will know how to hit the ball.

At the top, the elbow will be a bit away from you, but still comfortably in, generally pointing to the ground. The feeling will be one of compactness as your swing begins to become efficient.

Downswing

The downswing has no pre-determined plan; it is nothing more than a succession of movements which in the space of a second or two sees your clubhead impact the golf ball. But to get that clubhead to the ball there must, of course, be disciplined movement.

It has been said that there is no real top to the backswing, that the hands and club are still going back when the hips have started their move out of the way of the downswing. It seems, then, that the hips truly start the move in the other direction. This may be, but I try to have my hands, arms, shoulders all pulling down together. The precise flow is that of the hands being pulled down as the shoulders are turning and the hips are sliding, with all the movements synchronising. Our objective is not to prove what movement came first, but to suggest that you accept, in your own mind, the particular first movement that will get your body and hands in proper position to hit the ball long and consistently straight.

If you want distance, try for the late hit. That is, always get the clubhead to work behind the hands. If the hands lead the clubhead into the hitting area, the hit will be later, and the later the hit, the greater the distance.

Three faults can occur here. One is hitting too late, another is hitting too early. Too early means hitting from the top, invariably caused by rolling the wrists, and when the left hand overpowers the right coming down. The result is a hook or a pull, with the ball travelling to the right. Conversely, when you hit too late, the clubhead is delayed so the right hand leads the left by too much, there is a cutting action across the ball, and you slice, pushing or fading the ball to the left.

The third fault is an upset in rhythm, which might well be the real cause of the other two errors. In the downswing, the right hand is there to lead and guide the club. The hit itself is applied with the left, but remember that there is no conscious effort to think of either hand in particular. Both hands must work together as a unit, with neither dominating the other, causing a hit that is too early or too late.

The right arm continues on through almost to the completion of the follow through. There will be an obvious rolling action of the left hand over the right, but that is quite natural and you should not upset your swing by deliberately trying to stop this. Instead, pay attention to what the shoulders and left elbow must do to ensure distance with reliable accuracy.

Coming into the ball, the left shoulder stays behind and goes below the level of the right shoulder until, almost at impact, the shoulders will be in a line and at an angle of 30 degrees to the right of your target. Check this out carefully, because being aware of this will stop any tendency to move the left shoulder out over the line, changing the club's plane.

Be certain the left elbow brushes the left hip. The shoulder will then stay inside, and the plane of the swing and the squareness of the clubface will be assured. Checking the elbow will also help guide your hands in a fine arc, and you will be swinging correctly into and through the ball. Your swing will be compact.

The hips have moved considerably and quite fast and, as your stomach feels the contact of the ball, your hips are facing at an angle of 45 degrees away from the ball. This is the time for the left elbow to stay tucked well into the side, because it is a big help in preventing the shoulders from causing a slice or even a pull by turning away from the line. Remember to keep that left shoulder down and behind the ball for as long as possible. A left elbow that is in close helps more than just a little.

The more efficiently you attune your swing, the more power you are going to supply and the more distance you will get. Power is weight plus speed. Clubhead speed is generated by fast hand movement through the hitting area. It is important to get everything in correct position in that hitting area. Attention must be given to your shoulders, hands, hips and feet, all of which play a part in getting additional yardage off the tee. The rapid shift of weight moving forward on the downswing, together with maximum possible clubhead speed, is what gives distance off the tee.

After hitting the ball, the clubhead carries on through and continues straight towards the hole, with the arms and hands also going straight out after the ball. There should be no break in the elbows or the wrists in the early stages of the follow through. This continuity does not happen until the natural roll of the left hand over the right begins to occur. It actually takes place when the hands skip past at waist level. Let this happen as a result of your swing, rather than as a planned manoeuvre, because it will happen.

I like to keep the clubhead square to the line as long as I can after impact. The right elbow is forced to bend only after I am well into my follow through.

At the completion of the follow through it is important, as it is through the whole swing, to maintain good balance. All the weight will have moved to the outside of the right foot, and there will be no weight at all on the left foot, except that needed to balance.

Chapter Five

Woods

The driver

THE tee shot is, I feel, the most important shot in the game next to the putt. If you start the hole successfully with a good drive in or even near the position you decided in your mind as you lined up on the tee at the start of your round, you will be at least 25 per cent of the way to achieving what you set out to do. It is very important to have the tee shot in the middle of the fairway and not in the rough or hazard. For me, the fairway centre point, in most cases, gives a psychological advantage over opponents. However, there are some holes where a tee shot needs to be positioned perhaps to the left or to the right of centre in order to open up the green. But we are talking about the average hole on the average golf course, and the average handicap golfer with the emphasis naturally on all left-handers.

During my very early days as a professional, particularly in 1960-1962 and later into the 1970s I had a reputation as a poor driver; next to my bunker play that was, perhaps, the weakest part of my play. There were periods in between when I drove well, and combined with a good short game this won titles.

However, useful tips from Bob Toski in the mid 1960s, but more particularly a couple of sessions with Geneva based American professional Volker Krajewski in 1982 and again in 1983 have had a significant effect on my game. Now my drive has become perhaps the strongest part of my game and the percentage of fairways I have been hitting over the past couple of years has increased remarkably.

Naturally with long, well-placed drives I'm able to start each hole with confidence and, hopefully, turn these to advantage and win more events in the name of the lefties.

Volker Krajewski, the man who put me right, is a German by birth. He moved with his family to the United States in 1955 when he was 10 years old.

Following some success in junior golf, he was offered an athletic scholarship at the Ohio State University, followed by two years' service in Vietnam before he started playing golf for a living.

I met Krajewski through John Lister with whom he travelled on the American tour for some time. He now describes his lifestyle as that of a golf professional (teacher) after having earlier been both a golf professional and a professional golfer (tournament player).

"V.K." as he is known, refers to his period instructing me during the 1982 Open at Troon as a "consultation" rather than a lesson, because discussion on the basis of the swing — what, when, how and why — concerned both of us.

"My personal feeling is that what was happening to Bob and his game was occurring because of the weather — in particular, high winds and cold temperatures.

"At the time, Bob looked, and was, very much one sided. He seemed to be sitting on his right side. This caused the *left arm* to be over the *right arm,* creating a tension level to which he was not accustomed.

"Bob has always had an excellent set-up and one piece takeaway from the ball, but because of the tension forming in his arms, especially the left, he was actually cutting off his backswing and slightly closing the clubface causing his forearms and wrists to be also retarded.

"The *free flowing* arm motion that I remembered was no longer visible, the backswing was much shorter and tighter and in the end caused his upper torso to try and help move the club forward.

"I suggested that Bob *reduce* the *grip pressure* and *arm tension* a little and have the feeling that the arms were actually working independently of the body.

"The effect of this was that his left arm was immediately much more free and not causing the right arm to be pinned against the body on the takeaway. This allowed him to *let the club go back* instead of *forcing it back.* The clubface remained square and the backswing was unrestricted so the swing could take on a good shape once again, with the club in a good position at the top.

"Bob was now able to once again hit the shots he planned."

During the 1983 Swiss Open, "V.K." had another look at me after I had asked him to look at a particular move I had been making with my swing. "He had been working at keeping the club on line longer in the backswing. The problem with that particular action was that it caused the arms to tighten, inhibiting body rotation and eliminating shoulder turn. Hip rotation was also affected.

"After considerable discussion about that move," added "V.K.", "Charles freed up his arms, so his body could rotate."

The result was that shots started on line and stayed on line with some added height.

"In my view, he should have won the Swiss Open that year. The reason he missed out was disappointing putting."

In addition to the tips from "V.K.", I also have a new driver and a new shaft. This equipment makes all the difference to my long game. My confidence on the tee provides the incentive to do well and put big drives where I want them, setting the adrenalin flowing.

Feel is important in a golf club and for every player it is likely to be different. Some golfers, particularly those on a middle to high handicap, feel uncomfortable with the driver. They are likely to feel more at home with a No. 2 or No. 3 wood and though they will obviously be unable to get the same distance as they would if they were competent with the driver, they should find the other wood clubs enable them to retain a good degree of accuracy.

Through much of my professional career I was considered by other players and commentators to be a short hitter from the tee. But that's not 100 per cent correct, for in 1963 when I won the British Open at Royal Lytham and St Annes, it was not just my ability with my putter which won me the title. My driving was long and fairly straight. I hit the ball vast distances. In later years I did lose some distance — or was it the presence of "young giants", especially on the United States tour, hitting the ball out of sight which made it appear that way?

No matter, the fact is that for a period in my career during the 1970s, I was not long enough off the tee to match the American "powerhouses", hence my decision to campaign elsewhere.

Since talking with "V.K." and having him get me to loosen my grip on the club, I've again started hitting tee shots in the mould of my 1963 form at Houston and in the British Open, which in itself is perhaps amazing as I'm now 22 years older and on the verge of 50.

Indeed, I feel it is worth saying that friends, writers and broadcasters who have followed my game over the years have volunteered the view that in good conditions I am today hitting my tee shots some 20 to 25 yards (20 metres) longer than I was a decade or more ago. In other words, where in the early 1970s well hit drives were out to 230 yards (210 metres), I am today getting out to 250 yards (230 metres). At my age that is a bonus.

The driver is now one of the favoured clubs in my bag and on the Seniors' tour it will be a vital weapon in my armoury. If you are a regular No. 2 and No. 3 wood user and would like to achieve that vital extra distance, you should spend a little time in the pro shops looking for a No. 1 wood or driver and learn to use it well.

Your club professional is the person to set you on the right road, but, of course, you will need many hours of practice. At times you may become frustrated at not being able to master the "Big Fellow" Don't despair. Practice, so it is said, makes perfect — well almost!

Before you hit that first tournament or competition drive of the day, you should have visited the practice fairway for a warm up. Track and field athletes and tennis players among many other sportspeople don't step into the competitive arena without giving their muscles some toning. As a golfer, no matter at what level of competition, you are no different. You can't expect to start confidently if you are not in good condition.

It is said of golf that a well struck drive placed where you want it from the first tee is a good omen for the day ahead. I can't disagree with that.

In the warm up period before my first drive of the day, I will discuss the placement of the pin on the green with my caddy and consider the wind direction, for gusty conditions do affect the movement of a golf ball in the air.

Now that we have warmed up and know what lies ahead, it is into position on the tee. Note the position of the ball in relation to my feet as I line up (photograph A). It is actually positioned off the right heel or instep. The feet are about the width of the shoulders apart, while the hands are over the ball but slightly forward of the clubhead. Observe also the straight line extending up the shaft through my straight right arm. My weight balance is evenly distributed between both feet at this point.

Now that I'm lined up on the target and feeling comfortable, I can get on with the day's work with the takeaway, for once I'm into that there is no turning back.

Initially in the takeaway the club is extended away from the ball, low to the ground with hands and arms in control. As the club moves back, a weight shift starts on the left side, with the head also being tilted slightly to the left.

As my hands reach waist level the wrists start to cock and if the swing is correct the extension of the club will be good — about parallel with the ground and not in a steep angle as is often seen in the takeaway of long handicap players. Because of the almost level plane of the club at this point in the takeaway, the good extension of the hands and arms has forced the shoulders to start turning.

From waist level and back and up through the takeaway the trunk (shoulders and hips) has turned to its maximum, while the right knee is bending towards the ball. The wrists are continuing to cock although I do not have a big wrist break, preferring instead to have a firm grip for more control. At the top of my backswing my shoulders have turned at right angles to the ball, the hips are at 45 degrees, and the right knee has moved in and behind the ball. All these movements have caused the right heel to lift off the ground, with the weight predominantly on the left side. If I adopted a more flexible wrist action and lighter grip, I could get the club shaft to the parallel position which is favoured by some players.

Now, the downswing — the action — begins.

You will note in Photograph F that as I start down, there is a weight move from the left side to the right, the right heel is on the ground and the hip movement is going to the right, while my wrists remain cocked.

Through Photographs G, H and I, I am really into the action area. Photograph G shows the hips and shoulders turning to the right in that order, while in photograph H the wrists are beginning to uncock and my weight is moving rapidly onto the right foot. My left elbow is tucked into the body. In Photograph I, the club is gathering momentum as the wrists uncock and the hands move the club towards its maximum speed for impact. The left leg is moving to the right, causing the right side to clear and enable me to produce the power for long and, I hope, well placed drives.

Power is weight plus speed. To be sure of achieving power it is essential to get everything in the correct position. Close and careful attention must be given to so many things — shoulders, hands, hips and feet. Having precision in those areas should ensure maximum distance, coupled, perhaps, with a pushing action of the left foot which takes the weight off the left and moves it across to the right so the weight can be felt through the legs and into the shoulders. With this action you'll find that your left heel lifts up off the ground.

Photograph J shows the club speed just before impact. At this point in my swing, most of my weight is on the right side, which has cleared the shot. My right arm and right leg remain straight, as yours should be, and my eyes are glued to the ball. No head lifting here. Long handicap amateurs and others should not look up to see what's going to happen to the ball.

The follow through should happen automatically if you've been set up well from the outset.

After hitting the ball, the clubhead carries on through and continues straight towards the hole, with the player's arms and the hands also going out after the ball.

DRIVER — FRONT

A Address or stance position for the driver from the front. The ball is actually positioned off the right heel or instep. The feet are about the width of the shoulders apart. Note the straight line extending up the shaft through my straight right arm. My weight is evenly distributed between both feet.

B Start of the takeaway. The club is being extended away from the ball low to the ground with the hands and arms. Weight shift has started to the left side. Note that my head has tilted slightly to the left.

C My hands are now waist high, which is where the wrists should be as they start to cock. The extension of the club is good and different from high handicap players who at this stage have probably already picked up the club in a steeper angle with an early wrist cock. The extension of the hands and arms has forced the shoulders to start turning.

D The trunk (shoulders and hips) is now turning to its maximum, with the right knee bending towards the ball. The wrists are continuing to cock although as you will see in the next shot, I do not have a big wrist break, preferring, with my firm grip, to have more control.

E I am now at the top of my backswing. The shoulders have turned at right angles to the ball. The hips are at 45 degrees. The right knee has moved in and behind the ball. All these movements have caused the right heel to come off the ground. Weight is now predominantly on the left side. The club shaft is in the favoured or preferred parallel position.

F The start of the downswing with the weight moving from the left side to the right side. Note the right heel on the ground and hip movement towards the right. The wrists remain cocked.

G Note wrists are still fully cocked. The trunk is now twisting in reverse, with the hips back to square and the weight moving to the right side. In other words, the hips and shoulders are turning to the right in that order.

H At about this point in the downswing the wrists are beginning to uncock. The weight is moving rapidly to the right foot. Note the left elbow tucked into the body.

I The wrists are uncocking and the hands start to move the club at its maximum speed for impact. The left leg starts driving to the right with the right side clearing. This is where the *power* is produced.

J The clubhead is about to make contact with the ball. Most of the weight is now on the right side which has cleared the shot. Note the straight line of the right leg and right arm. My eyes are glued to the ball.

K This shot shows clearly how I keep my eyes fixed tirmiy on the spot where the ball was on the tee even though I am into the follow through. The hit is noticeably against a *firm* right side. Again note the straight right arm and also the almost straight left arm. This helps to keep the clubface square at impact.

L Further into the follow through, and the hips and shoulders are still turning with a full extension of the arms. Note the straight left arm and also the position of the left shoulder below the right. The force of the hit has caused the clubface to close with the left hand turning over the right.

M By this point in the follow through most high handicappers have broken their left arm at the elbow. My right arm is beginning to break but the left is fully extended. The head is coming up with the turning of the shoulders.

N A good, high finish with the hands completing the follow through. All the weight is now on the right foot and side, and the left toe helps maintain good balance. Most high handicappers will at this point have the left foot flat on the ground in a "fall back off-balance situation"

O The stance or address position for the driver from the rear. The weight is evenly distributed between the heels and toes while the feet, hips and shoulders are square to the intended line. The knees are slightly flexed and the back straight. The ball is positioned a comfortable distance from the feet. Note the gap between my hands and thighs.

P The club is started back, with the hands, arms, shoulders and hips in that order. Here only the hands and arms have moved.

Q The shoulders and hips are now starting to move with the extension of the club back from the ball. The right shoulder is turning underneath the chin, causing the right knee to start moving forward.

R Nearing the top of the takeaway with the left elbow coming away and the shoulders and hips almost completing the wind up.

S I'm at the top of my takeaway, with the left knee as it was at address and the right knee bent towards the ball allowing a full turn of hips and shoulders. I have a fairly upright swing which forces the left elbow away from my body. The club shaft at the top should be pointing parallel to the target.

T The start of the downswing showing a movement to the right with the hips turning and leading the shoulders and arms. The left elbow is coming into the body.

U The right side is clear and the wrists are starting to uncock, allowing maximum use of hands for accelerating the clubhead. The left heel is starting to push off the ground for maximum weight shift.

V Almost at impact with the ball. The left elbow is close to my body, and you will see that my shoulders are in line with the target and the hips cleared at about 30 degrees. The eyes remain glued to the ball.

W Just after impact, with the head still down and the club staying on the line for as long as possible. The right hip has moved out of the way to the right to allow the hands and arms to continue through and towards the target.

X The left shoulder continues to stay down and under the chin during the extension after impact.

Y The left arm is fully extended for a good, high follow through. Very few high handicappers would get the clubhead this high coming through.

Z The finish of the swing. All the weight is on the right foot, with the left toe on the ground to maintain balance.

Every golfer likes to hit drives out of sight. But that's just not possible. Long hitting is achieved through weight plus speed but the secret is to get your golfing body in trim. Your muscles should be finely tuned by exercise and, of course, hours upon hours of practice.

The golfer who plays only once or twice weekly will rarely attain regular, long, accurate driving unless those periods of preparation have been put in on the practice fairway. If you are a weekend golfer, I suggest you work at what you've been taught, remembering always to: take the clubhead back in a long arc; you don't necessarily have to have a long backswing, but if possible it ought to reach the horizontal when at the top or close to it.

Learn also to develop clubhead speed by moving the hands through the hitting area at a fast clip.

The weekend golfer should learn to hit up against a very solid right side. Everything on the right must be as firm as you can get it at impact — your right arm, right elbow and right leg.

After impact, try to get a very high finish, by keeping the left shoulder down and under until you feel it starting to pull your head around and up to watch the flight of the ball.

Woods, especially the driver, are used for distance. The driver is the club for tee shots but it should not be chosen as a matter of course for all tee shots on holes which normally call for the use of a wood.

The driver is for distance alone and if you feel you cannot get the accuracy and placement needed for good scoring, you should use a No. 3 or 4 wood or even a long iron.

In the 1963 British Open play-off, I put my driver away on several occasions, preferring instead to use my No. 3 wood. I scored under par on two of the three occasions when I chose that particular club.

When using the driver, tee the ball fairly high because it must be swept off the tee. No contact is made with the ground. The driver is the only club where no divot is taken, although I have seen some long handicappers doing the odd bit of "gardening" on tees from time to time.

SUMMARY

* Because this club can be difficult to master, think carefully about the hole you are going to play before taking the driver from your bag. Only use the driver when you feel confident of hitting the fairway.
* Stance and grip are orthodox, with the ball positioned just inside a line back to the right heel or instep.
* Keep the club extended long and low to the ground at the start of the takeaway.
* A full swing is required with a maximum turn of the shoulders and hips in the backswing.
* The first movement of my downswing is started by the hips, with a weight move from the left to the right side. The hands automatically start working in unison with the hip action and uncocking of the wrists follows. It is important not to hurry your swing. The action you've worked on with your professional should ensure a smooth result, if you've put into practice what you've been taught.

Fairway Woods

From the driver we move on to the fairway woods, the No. 2, the No. 3, the No. 4 and No. 5 and for some players even a No. 6 or No. 7, two clubs which are now widely manufactured and which are increasingly popular with golfers who find they are unable to use the long or mid irons.

Of these woods the No. 2 is a most difficult one to master and the most dangerous for the weekender to use. On the other hand, it is the club to give the maximum fairway distance if the lie is near perfect; it is also the club that can be used when the driver goes sour. The No. 2 has about 3 degrees more loft and can get the ball out almost as far as the driver if you hit it correctly. In my experience the best choice of a fairway wood under most circumstances is more often the No. 3 or No. 4 wood. These clubs require more of a downward descending blow to strike the ball, than is called for with the driver. You should brush the ground, even take a bit of a divot, but nowhere near as much as you would when using an iron.

With all fairway woods, play the ball a little further back in your stance as you move down from the driver, which is played from just inside your right heel.

The woods are the longest clubs in your bag. This length means that clubhead speed is easier to develop. Although some of them have less loft than the long irons, they are, because of their added length, able to propel the ball in a higher trajectory. They are often ideal to use to a green around 195 to 225 yards (178 to 205 metres) away and protected in front by a hazard. They are also good clubs to use out of some types of rough when the grass is light enough to allow the clubhead to move through.

Overall, I feel that the No. 3 wood is perhaps the most versatile of the fairway woods because it is a tool which most handicap golfers should be able to handle without too much trouble. For the medium and long handicappers — and they are in the majority — the No. 3 wood is the most suitable club for those fairway shots up to around 200 yards (183 metres). It is not a club for great distances. Instead, it is a weapon which if used correctly can help reduce those handicap figures.

The No. 4 wood is another of those clubs which if mastered can become a stroke saver and make the game more enjoyable. Because of its construction — greater loft in the head — you are able to get the ball to rise faster, with more backspin, reducing the possibility of hooked or sliced shots. Like the No. 3 wood, it is not a club which will carry the ball vast distances.

The No. 4 and 5 woods are good for extracting shots from semi or light rough.

As you learn to play and control these clubs, it is important that you work out just how well you can hit particular shots and when on course work within your skills and experience.

The lie of the ball is, of course, important no matter what club you are playing. Never take a fairway wood from your bag until you have carefully considered the position of the ball on the ground. If it is sitting up well, study the distance and terrain ahead and then go for the wood you know will do for you what you require of it.

If, however, the ball is buried in the rough or maybe even in a fairway bunker, you may find it better to play for position rather than distance. In such cases use an iron.

* As with all clubs a good fairway wood shot should be smooth and slow, with the takeaway and follow through in the same mould as for the driver.
* Like all shots there should be no rush. The golfer who adopts a hit and run approach because not enough time has been set aside for the round, will almost certainly run into problems. Remember to think . . . slow takeaway . . . don't hurry . . . and keep your head still and accelerate through the ball.

My average wood distances are:

Driver	250 yards	(230 metres)
No. 2 Wood	240 yards	(220 metres)
No. 3 Wood	230 yards	(210 metres)
No. 4 Wood	220 yards	(200 metres)
No. 5 Wood	210 yards	(192 metres)

I personally carry a No. 1, 3 and 4 wood in my bag. I do not use a No. 2 or 5 wood.

As a guide, a good player will use each of the above mentioned clubs for distances indicated in average conditions.

Chapter Six

Long and mid irons

Long irons

STANDING on tees and in fairways of courses all over the world during the past 25 years, I have heard spectators commenting: "What a beautiful shot into that green. It must have been at least 200 yards. His ball must be close to the hole."

I enjoy nothing more than watching tournament golf and seeing a good player hit those long irons with marksman-like accuracy. Having had the good fortune at times to have been on the receiving end of spectator applause, I think there is something very special about a long iron hit into the heart of the green with the ball finishing close to the pin.

You can learn to play such shots.

The long irons are the No. 2, No. 3 and No. 4 and for the few players who have it in their bag, the No. 1 iron. I have never carried a No. 1 iron, preferring instead the No. 4 wood.

The long irons are perhaps the most difficult clubs to use. Many players find it hard to get the ball into the air. To get the ball up, you must hit down and through the shot. This may seem contradictory, but golf is in many ways a game of opposites. This piece of the game is one of them.

The higher handicap golfer tends to hit the ball off the back foot with the club sweeping up from the ball. Although the driver and to a lesser degree, the fairway woods are hit with a sweeping action, it is essential to hit the ball a descending blow with all iron shots, taking a divot after the ball, and allowing the loft of the club and the backspin to get the ball into the air.

As golfers become more proficient they tend to also become more adventurous and are prepared to use clubs which previously stayed in their bags. These include the No. 1 and No. 2 irons.

Practice is important and golfers should be satisfied only when they can hit a target with some regularity. Besides being stroke savers, the properly hit long iron sets the adrenalin flowing and gives a sweet feeling that you cannot get from any other group of clubs. Though many golfers experience periods of conflict with those weapons, perseverance and practice can result in real proficiency with the long irons.

Properly executed long iron shots are, like all shots with other clubs, stroke savers if used correctly.

In the photographs I am using a No. 4 iron. In Photograph A, my stance and address position is somewhat narrower than that used when playing the driver. This is because the club is shorter.

The takeaway is, of course, slow and deliberate. In Photograph E — top of the backswing — there is very little difference in appearance from that of the driver. The body is in full turn and perfectly balanced for the downswing and action — contact with the ball and follow through.

It takes only a few seconds from the time you start your backswing until you come back down and finish the shot. But in that time you can get into all sorts of trouble if you hurry the shot.

Ask yourself if it takes less time to get to the top of your swing than it does to return

A This is my stance or address position for a No. 4 iron. The stance is somewhat narrower than for the driver, and the ball is positioned inside the heel. The weight is evenly distributed. The hands are ahead of the clubhead.

B Backswing starting with hands and arms in good extension.

C The hands are waist high and shoulders have turned; the hips are also starting to turn.

D Three-quarters of the way back with most of my weight now on the left foot.

E Top of the swing, which is very little different from the driver, with a full turn and wind-up.

F Starting down with the hips uncoiling.

G The weight is moving to the right and I am set for the hit.

H Just before impact: the hands lead the clubhead for a descending blow.

I Just after impact: the clubface remains square for as long as possible after impact.

J Good extension through the ball. Note the hand position.

K Full finish with hands high. The body faces the target area. The balance is good with the weight on the right side as with all shots.

LONG AND MID IRONS — REAR

L The stance remains square to the target for long and medium irons.

M Start of takeaway.

N The body is starting to wind up around the head.

O Wrists are now starting to cock. The left elbow is tucked into the body for as long as possible.

P The top of the swing with a good full turn of the hips and shoulders. The club is in a position similar to that used for the driver. With the full turn of the shoulders in my upright swing, the left elbow comes away from the side.

Q Coming down and into the ball. My knees are bent and wrists still cocked. My left elbow is back in against the body, helping to keep the club on the correct downward plane.

R Moments before impact, with the wrists uncocking for maximum leverage and power.

S Just after impact, with shoulders still in line with the target area.

T The club extends and remains on target with the eyes still glued to the ground.

U Well into follow through with the shoulders pulling the head up.

V Good balance at the finish with all the weight on the right foot.

to the ball. If your answer is yes, then your backswing is too fast. This is a common error. Slow down. A gentle but still controlled takeaway is required.

Over the years I have developed the feel of staying on the same line going back as I come down into the ball. This has been important in helping me develop a good rhythm.

Don't be afraid of your long irons, in particular the No. 2 and No. 3. They are not mavericks as I've heard some players suggest. With practice, determination and concentration you will master these clubs and get more enjoyment out of your golf.

For the middle handicap golfers and maybe the high single figure players too, the length of a No. 2 iron shot should be about 190 yards (175 metres) under good conditions. Sometimes the ball may fly a little further, depending on the swing and set up of the player. The average golfer's distance for the No. 3 iron should be in the 180 yards (165 metres) range. For the No. 4 iron, your expectation should be around the 170 yards (155 metres).

For all clubs, good timing is necessary for good results, but time is perhaps a little more important for these long irons.

Mid irons

The middle, or as they are popularly referred to, the mid irons, are the No. 5, No. 6 and No. 7. For some golfers, these clubs will not be as efficient as the shorter irons, but they have certainly been good to me. There have been occasions during my career when these mid irons have meant the difference between winning and finishing among the also-rans.

Back in 1962 I played a great No. 5 iron into a par five, the first hole of a play off in the Swiss Open. The execution of this shot enabled me to one putt to take the title. Victory was certainly sweet and made all those long hours of practice with that club suddenly seem worth while.

Six years later it was the turn of the No. 7 iron to not only delight me but to also bring smiles to the face of my bank manager. At the final hole of the 1968 Canadian Open, I put a No. 7 iron just 20 inches (50 centimetres) from the pin, under pressure, then sank the putt to close out Jack Nicklaus.

Because of their higher loft and shorter shaft length, the mid irons will have a narrower arc, and as the ball is positioned roughly between the right heel and the centre of the stance, a more downward blow results. The backswing is not deliberately shortened, nor is the body turn or weight shift restricted.

There is no change in rhythm and balance, but knowing how to swing these clubs is not always enough. You must also consider the type of fairway, the lie and the weather.

From a tight lie, use at least one club longer than normal because in going after the ball, you will create more backspin than usual. This will reduce the distance. If the ball is in a very fluffy lie, where the grass can get between it and the clubface, the reverse takes place and you will get maximum distance with little backspin. Compensate for this loss of backspin by using a shorter club, because you can expect the ball to fly.

Hitting out of rough produces the same type of uncontrolled shot. When the rough is deep, always aim to just get out. Never try for the miracle of hitting the ball over water, under a tree or clearing a trap. Instead, play it safe — back onto the fairway — and hope for a chip and one putt for your par.

Many times during my career I have faced this situation. The most memorable was in the 1963 British Open which I won. On the 24th hole of the play off, a par four of 466 yards (428 metres), I hooked my drive into the right hand rough, leaving no alternative but to get it safely out to avoid losing strokes. I used a No. 5 iron from the rough and then placed what I termed a "recovery wedge" five feet (1.5 metres) from the pin and sank the putt. It was a scrambling par, but it was better than a bogey!

I've read and heard it said that if a golfer can't get results with a No. 5 iron he can't play golf. These harsh words are not designed to build confidence. However, don't be put off by them if at the present time you are unable to hit a No. 5 iron well.

Regular consultations and lessons with your professional will soon get you hitting this club well and you should be able to achieve distances of around 160 yards (145 metres) with the No. 5 down to around 140 yards (128 metres) with the No. 7.

Because of the higher loft and shorter length, these clubs produce a slightly shorter backswing, with a steeper arc producing a more downward blow on the ball. Other than those few points, there are no differences in swing, rhythm and balance with these clubs compared with the long irons.

By keeping to the basics of the swing, with a good stance, slow takeaway and full hip and shoulder turn on the way through, you will find yourself really enjoying your game with every iron in the bag.

As a guide these are my average hitting distances for the irons:

No. 2	200 yards (183 metres)
3	190 yards (174 metres)
4	180 yards (165 metres)
5	170 yards (155 metres)
6	160 yards (145 metres)
7	150 yards (136 metres)
8	140 yards (128 metres)
9	130 yards (119 metres)
Wedge	120 yards (110 metres)
Sand Wedge	90 yards (82 metres)

Chapter Seven

Short irons

NEXT to my putting, my short iron play has been the best part of my game over the years.

These clubs include the No. 8 and No. 9 irons, the wedge and sand wedge which, of course, are used from varying distances. In short iron play, the use of the wedge and sand wedge is different from chipping with those two clubs. This chapter refers to the use of those clubs for full shots; chipping is covered in Chapter 9.

The short irons should be a deadly part of every golfer's arsenal. Birdies are more likely to be made with these clubs than with the medium or long irons.

Because of the nature of the clubs and their purpose — chipping and putting — the short iron game can be practised regularly. Large areas are not required for those full shots.

The full sand wedge is a shot I use often; in fact one of these clubs rarely lasts me more than two seasons. Continuous practice soon wears out the club.

I used a sand wedge to good effect during the 1978 Air New Zealand Open at Titirangi in New Zealand. As I teed off on the last hole, I needed a birdie three to win. A good tee shot saw me positioned 80 yards (73 metres) from the pin — a distance which is by no means a full wedge for many tournament players. For me it was a full sand wedge and fortunately my execution was excellent. The ball came to rest about 18 inches (45 centimetres) from the hole. I made the putt, and victory was a great thrill, not only because it was my first win in four years, but it was also in my own country and before some of the largest galleries ever seen on a New Zealand golf course.

I enjoy playing my short irons, indeed, almost every shot from about 100 yards (90 metres) into the green, including sand, rough and apron, I make with a wedge. I would have to be faced with a shot of 130 to 140 yards (120 to 130 metres) to consider the No. 8 iron. This is about the distance from which I would also use a No. 7 iron, but only if the lie were tight, or if I was playing from very hard ground. But I would not hit the shot firmly; I would concentrate on contacting the ball and hitting it crisply to produce a lot of backspin. I would pitch this shot right up to the hole, knowing it should bite very quickly.

If, however, at the same distance the ball were sitting up on a fluffy grass I would take the No. 9 iron and plan to hit the ball well short of the pin, knowing it would come down and keep rolling towards the hole.

To be successful with your short irons you must know your own abilities. While there will be some overlapping of distance with each club, it is always best to let the club do the full job. Hit your shot with the well grooved swing you have worked at perfecting and you should get the results you want. If you have doubts about the outcome of your shot with the No. 9 iron, turn to the wedge. I've found it great for the short approaches.

The wedge is an American invention, credited with helping players to make the very low scores which have become part of modern golf, at professional and amateur levels. Better equipment generally plus more attention to technique have contributed to better scoring, but the wedge has helped everyone.

The wedge is made for a purpose; use it only for that purpose and you will probably be happy with the results.

At address for the short irons, the feet are closer together than for the medium or long irons, but not as close as for the chip. (See Chapter 6.)

Photograph A shows that the ball is positioned about halfway between my feet, while my right arm runs through in a straight line from the shoulder down the shaft to the clubhead. The takeaway is similar to the longer iron, with a good arm extension which ensures that at the top of my swing I am almost as far back as for the longer irons and in a good position for a smooth downswing to impact with the ball. It is important that as you contact the ball, the clubhead is descending to take a large divot in front of the ball. A properly executed shot will have a natural loft; the club is designed for that purpose.

The follow through with the short irons is similar to the others in your bag — a good extension keeping your head down. Not until the closing stages of the follow through should the shoulders start bringing the head up. If you try to come up too quickly, the ball will fly away and end up far from where you want it. You must stay on line to avoid problems. As with the driver, a good finish is required on all full shots.

The ball is closer to the feet than for the longer clubs but at a distance which allows freedom to swing without the body impeding the shot and affecting the swing.

Some golfers tend to adopt a pronounced crouch when playing their short irons. This is not necessary. Your set up must be comfortable while keeping to the basic rules for other clubs in the bag.

SHORT IRONS — FRONT

A Front view of the address for the short iron. At address for the short iron the feet are closer together than for long or medium irons but not as close as for the chip. The ball is positioned towards the centre of the feet. Note the straight line down my right arm and the club shaft. Weight is evenly distributed.

B Takeaway of short iron is similar to the long iron with good extension.

C Three-quarters of the way back with the weight now on the left foot; the body is still turning.

D At the top and almost as far back as for the long iron. The shoulder and hip turn is good with nothing restricted.

E This could be a long iron as everything is in the same position. The legs are pushing the weight from the left foot to the right side.

F Just before impact. Because of the shorter shaft in this iron the clubhead comes at the ball on a steeper angle or descends downward taking a large divot ahead of the ball. Do not try to pick up the ball; let the loft of the club do it.

G Moments after impact with the hit against the right side.

H The follow through — a good extension with head down.

I Shoulders bringing the head up; left arm still straight.

J As with the driver, a good finish is required on all full shots. The weight is on the right foot.

K Short iron shot from the rear showing the feet slightly open. Otherwise the hips and shoulders are square with the line, while the ball is closer to the feet but still allowing freedom to swing the hands and club. Posture is the same as for the driver. Some people crouch needlessly over the short irons.

L The early stages of the takeaway, with feet and shoulders just starting to turn.

M The hands reach waist height before any thought of wrist lock.

N Two-thirds of the way back.

O At the top for the short iron with a full turn of hips and shoulders. The only time the turn is restricted is with a half or three-quarter shot.

P Have you seen this picture before? It would be any club from wedge to driver.

Q Contacting the ball on the clubface first, and about to take a divot after the ball.

R Just after impact. The ball is on the way. I am still behind the shot with good balance.

S Extending through the ball after impact.

T Completion of the follow through which is almost the same as the driver.

Chapter Eight

Chipping

A real stroke saver — that is how I regard chipping. No matter what level of the game you play, you are going to miss a lot of greens, some by a long way; others will be close. But if you can get up and down for one putt consistently from around 30 yards (28 metres) you will lower your handicap and come closer to winning events.

I use three clubs for chipping, each of them for shots of varying distances. Terrain and situation are also factors.

The sand wedge I use from about 90 yards (85 metres) into the green edge where it is necessary to land the ball on the green. It is important in chipping to land the ball on the green wherever possible and to avoid longish grass close to the greenside. Unreliable bounces can happen if your line to the hole is not level, and if your chip shot hits short of the planned drop zone.

I use the wedge from about 90 to 120 yards (85 to 110 metres). At times I also use it for chipping close to and around the green.

Surprisingly, perhaps, I also use a third club for close to green running shots, but using a totally different technique. The club in question is the No. 4 iron.

Pitch shot

With the delicate pitch shots using the sand wedge from about 30 to 40 yards (28 to 35 metres) from the pin, or perhaps the little flip over a trap, finesse and timing are needed. This is a shot that can be developed only through a lot of practice. It needs time to master — if you are able to. Take time to get the feel that must go into its execution, and time to gain confidence in yourself.

For this shot, I suggest you open your stance somewhat. Have your feet fairly close together, knees relaxed and bent in quite a lot. Move your right toe towards the hole a bit, and play the ball approximately at the centre of your stance. How you play the shot depends on the type of lie. If it is neither good nor bad, use very little hip and shoulder movement, with little pivot and no conscious effort to turn away from the ball. Your concern for balance might be minimised; just keep it more towards the heels than to the toes, a movement which encourages the blade to move outside the proper line, upsetting your accuracy. Make a great effort to keep your tempo even. Then it is just a matter of taking the club back, breaking the wrists fairly sharply immediately in the backswing (but without any further wrist movement) and from there it is mainly an arm and hand movement.

The clubhead is taken back normally, slowly, but returns to contact the ball quite sharply, continuing through and finishing with a restricted follow through. There is no need to think about finishing high.

An exception is the shot out of a grassy lie, or from lush clover, or if you are in long rough. These situations call for hitting through the ball and taking the clubhead up a little more, making certain that you first get the club going through the grass. When the lie is a bit bare, you have to hit down on the ball with very little follow through.

If nothing is in your line but fairway and

little or no rise, use a less lofted club to chip and run.

All the practice time you can spare to learn this shot will reward you with more pars and birdies. Confidence and ability in this shot means you can recover even if you do miss the green with your approach. A pitch to within two or three feet (60 to 90 centimetres) from the pin will save many shots. This is not too much to strive for. In time you'll find it pleasurable to pitch those short shots directly at the target. Soon your main concern will be to produce enough elevation to keep the ball moving actively, over any possible trouble areas, and to drop it down on a predetermined spot on the green so it will stop somewhere near the hole. This is self-discipline and satisfaction at its best.

Pitch and run

For the pitch and run shot from 5 to 10 yards (5 to 10 metres) of the fringe, I use a wedge. Keep this shot simple. If possible, use a putter. You'll know when it is feasible to do so; when there is not too much apron between the ball and the green, when the grass is not too high, when the grain is not against you, and when the lie is good. Otherwise you will undoubtedly choose between a lofted club such as a No. 9 or a wedge, or a club with a straighter face, such as a No. 6 or No. 7 iron. With the former, pick a spot or draw an imaginary circle of any diameter about two-thirds of the way to the pin; stroke the ball to this spot and expect it to roll the remaining one-third distance. With the No. 6 or No. 7 iron, plan on the ball's landing on a target about one-third of the way to the cup and rolling the remaining two-thirds. The execution or set up of the pitch and run is similar to the pitch with the sand wedge except that the hands and the club will move a considerably shorter distance and the loft on the club is less. Make sure your knees are relaxed, and do not stiffen your body so your hands are under strain in taking the club back and returning it to the ball.

Run shots

When I can't use the putter I go with the No. 4 iron. The method of execution is dramatically different from the use of the wedge. With the No. 4 iron I use the same grip and stance as with my putter, and employ the same stroke as with the putter — that is with no wrist or body movement. Only the arms and shoulders swing the club.

It is possible to use the No. 5, No. 6 or No. 7 irons for this shot. However, I find it easier to practise with just one club than with a lot of them. I learn how this club will react; I can quickly get the feel for the shot and can approach the testing situation the same way each time.

Whichever club you prefer, follow a plan and do not compromise with this system. Soon you'll have the shot under control and, like a lengthy putt, you can expect to make a few now and then.

Club selection is a matter of personal preference. For the weekend golfer I recommend the rolling chip shot using a No. 4 iron. However, remember with all clubs, whenever possible, to chip to land the ball on the green which, as you know, offers a more reliable bounce and allows for quite a bit of roll.

When to use the putter

These rules are standard, not only to encourage you into proper club selection, but also to guide you into executing the shot with a plan. This means that if you have too much fairway or apron to contend with, the No. 4 iron is not the club to use. Even if it is closer, it doesn't naturally follow that the No. 4 iron is the proper weapon. Try the putter.

The rules for putting on the apron of the green are commonsense ones: do not use this nearly straight bladed club when the grain is against you, or when the grass is too high, or when the green is too slick, or when you have too much apron to traverse. Otherwise employ the usual putting procedures.

The tough grass-bunker shot

The most difficult pitch shot is the one that has the ball nestled in heavy grass not more than a few feet from the putting surface. My choice for this situation is the trusty sand wedge, hitting into the ball not unlike the method used in a sand trap. Although it might be odd to see someone taking a full cut at such a short shot, it is about the only way to extricate the ball.

I hit in behind the ball, keeping the clubhead moving, letting the flange at the bottom of the club cut through the grass, getting the club under the ball, which pops up and out. The blade is closed a trifle to prevent the flange from making the club bounce off the ground into the belly of the ball. This is not just a hit and stop shot. A full swing, depending on the distance required, and a follow through are essential.

CHIPPING

A Stance for chip and run shot with No. 4 iron from the front.

B The No. 4 iron is used also for chip and run at the start of the backswing. As with the putt, the wrists are locked, only the arms and shoulders have moved in the pendulum action. The length of the backswing depends on the distance required.

C The No. 4 iron chip and run at the end of the follow through. With a pendulum action the follow through has been extended more than in the backswing. Unlike the putt, the legs have moved into the shot.

D Another view of the stance with the No. 4 iron run shot and using the Funk Setup Master. The grip is almost the same as for the putter, with a reverse overlap, and the hands are comfortably down the shaft. The address is very similar to that used for the putter.

E The No. 4 iron run shot from another angle. Because of the length of the shaft and the lie of the club, the ball is positioned further from the feet than with the putter. Otherwise the stance is the same — square feet, knees, hips and shoulder.

F The address for the wedge chip. The stance for this shot from the angle provides for a slightly open stance. The hands are close into the body but still allow room for freedom of movement. The stance must be comfortable with the knees flexed and the weight distributed evenly between the heels and toes, assuring good balance.

G Front view of the address for the wedge chip. The grip has not changed, although I often remove my right-hand glove for better feel. The hands are positioned ahead of the clubhead and the feet are close together. There are only about 12 inches (30 centimetres) between each foot. My knees are well flexed with the weight favouring my right side. The ball is positioned just forward of a centre line between the feet.

H The sand wedge chip. I use this club to carry the ball on to the green and stop it near the hole. A wedge would take the ball rolling on well past my target area. With the sand wedge the ball will go higher and a bigger swing is required than with the wedge. Note that only the arms and hands have moved the club, with very little shoulder and leg movement.

I The sand wedge after impact: you will see that my head is still down. The position is the same as with the wedge chip from the front.

J Finish of follow through of sand wedge shot: there is a good, high follow through on this pitch of 25 yards. The body is relaxed. Good balance is a feature of the finish. The weight is mostly on the right leg.

K Wedge chipping: This is a very good photograph because it shows the ball in the air. It also shows that my head is still fixed in the address position. Although there was little body movement in the backswing, you will see how the legs have moved into the shot, allowing me to keep my hands ahead of the club. The line-up is straight from the shaft into the straight right arm.

L The sand wedge: after impact. This photograph shows almost the same position as Photograph I but is from the back.

M The sand wedge backswing: The technique is basically the same as for the wedge. The stance is open, and the arms and wrists have moved. There is no need for any body turn from this distance. Note also the almost square blade to the line of flight.

N The sand wedge: Finish of follow through. Note position of the ball for this lofted chip shot. The head has now moved to follow the flight of the ball. The weight is almost totally on the right side and right foot. Note also the position of the left foot.

Chapter Nine

Trap or sand shots

IF there has been one part of my game which has caused me problems over the years it has been in bunkers. Sand shots and Bob Charles just haven't clicked. In fact it is probably true that my lack of perfection in the execution of bunker shots has cost me some tournament victories and certainly prevented me from realising my full potential, particularly in the United States.

The reason for my inability to play out of bunkers probably dates back to my childhood when I started playing golf on a course without any sand-traps. Even when I was a teenager, the course I played on most of the time had only two holes with sand bunkers. This meant I spent little time trying to perfect that part of my game.

In spite of that early absence of practice, I have done a lot of work with my sand clubs and now regard myself as at least proficient.

The first requirement for successful bunker play is a sand wedge which has a deep flange on the sole so the club will bounce through the sand in an explosion type of shot beneath the ball, lofting it up, out and onto the green, from a greenside bunker with the ball sitting up well on top of the sand.

I am able to play out of some types of sand better than others. The seaside links of Great Britain, including Royal Lytham and St. Annes and St. Andrews, have natural sand. With these I find I have some compatibility. But the bunkers on most of the American courses on which I've played have artificial sand. For these I have no love at all. In these bunkers the ball tends to bury itself in the fluffy sand. An imbedded ball is never easy to play.

The only way to any success with bunker play is through hours and hours of practice and learning correct technique.

Though I have some misgivings about bunker play, I do know that confidence is essential. Always step into the bunker in a positive mood, telling yourself, "I can play this shot well." Without confidence in bunker play, or any other part of the game, you cannot even hope to have any success at all.

I experienced this confidence in New Zealand in 1974, during what was then the City of Auckland Classic. Naturally, every sportsman and woman enjoys winning in their home country and as I stood on the tee preparing to play the final hole, I learned from a progress scoreboard that a par four was needed if I was to salute the judge. The last hole at The Grange course requires a perfect drive to avoid trees on both sides of the fairway. My drive was perfect and I was well set up to put my second on the green. Alas, I was off line and into a greenside bunker which was far from where I had planned to be and not where I wanted to be. There are no second chances in this game of golf so I had to find every ounce of confidence possible in order to get down in two from 50 feet (15 metres) to take away first prize. For someone with a dislike of bunkers I played one of those great shots, putting the ball just a foot from the cup.

The sand wedge is a unique club, tailor-made to solve most of the sand trap problems. The wide flange is specially designed to let the club bounce through the sand; the thick sole prevents the club from becoming embedded. Its invention in the 1930s has helped to lower golf scores. It is a definite asset, because it is the proper tool for the job, increasing your chances of getting the ball out of the hazard and relatively close to the pin. I know from experience that if you walk into the bunker with the thought of just getting out, the chances are you'll do just that, and only that. Since I have adopted positive thinking, things have changed for me, and I feel that when in a trap I've got a good chance of getting close to the pin, that I'm going to get out and down in one putt every time I walk into — and quickly out of — the trap.

For the shot that requires high loft and enough distance to travel from 10 to 30 feet (3 to 10 metres), play the ball off the right heel using a very open stance with the clubface open as well. Your feet should be fairly close together — not more than 18 inches (45 centimetres) apart.

Dig your feet in very firmly, because your stance must be secure, and you can also feel and gauge the consistency of the sand. The move away from the ball does not need a very big hip turn — only about a three-quarter swing — as it is mainly a shoulder and arm movement.

The club comes straight back from the ball with an early wrist break. The tempo should be relatively slow and evenly paced going back, and smooth and firm going into the ball. Hit the sand about 1½ inches (4 centimetres) behind the ball, continuing into a full follow through. As with all shots it is essential not to quit on the shot as the club enters the sand. Above all, keep the swing smooth and rhythmical.

When you need more distance, move your body to the left, towards the target. In other words, square your stance and also square the clubface. This change in address position also changes the plane of the swing and takes away the cutting action, resulting in a fairly high, lofted shot that will roll. This is about the only safe way to hit from a place in a trap quite removed from the pin that may be tucked up in the far corner, or on the top half of a large, two-level, undulating, uphill green.

The buried lie when the ball plops into heavy sand, making for itself a hole slightly larger than the ball itself, is not as difficult as it first appears. Don't panic. This ball can be popped out with less brute strength than you may think. Play the ball in the centre of the stance, with the blade closed and hands well ahead of the clubface. This will move the flange, created to bounce off the sand in a normal trap shot, further behind the club's leading edge, and will allow the clubface to continue down and through with the flange out of the way.

The sand, which appears to have a solid hold on the ball, can be put to use. When the clubhead makes contact with it about 1½ inches (3.75 centimetres) behind the ball, it creates a sort of wall that forces the ball up and out. After the hit, the clubhead follow through will be restricted by the extra depth of sand taken, and the ball will pop out rather low and with roll. Allow for this, because there is little that can be done to counteract it.

A Address position with the weight fairly even. Make sure your feet are dug in to stop the possibility of slipping and, of course, for successful execution of the shot.

B Start of takeaway.

C Top of backswing. Keep it short for control. Note the good shoulder turn with restricted hip turn.

D Just before impact. Wrists are uncocking, legs and arms are driving forward. Note my bent right knee.

E Moments after impact, with head down and legs relaxed. The ball has risen steeply.

F Finish of the swing. As for all shots, I display a good follow through and balance. These are essential for good results.

G Another view of the address position. My stance is very open with feet, hips and shoulders.

H The takeaway with open clubface and early wrist cock.

I Top of the swing with good shoulder turn.

J Just before impact with the weight moving into the right side. The knees are flexed.

K Moments after impact with the right side clearing and the head still down.

L Completion of follow through with all the weight on the right side. There is no attempt to quit on this shot.

Chapter Ten

The putter

FROM the time of my first important tournament victory, the 1954 New Zealand Open Championship, I established myself as a better than average putter with an ability to read greens. Other golfers wondered if I had some inner power that gave me an advantage. My success on the greens is the result of a good, early grounding and many hours of practice on all types of surfaces.

To me, the putter is a veritable life-line. It won for me tournaments when I was an amateur and also the play-off in the 1963 British Open Championship which I regard as the highlight of my career. In the play-off against American Phil Rodgers for that title, I played the two extra rounds in 69 and 71 for a total of 140; Phil scored 148. The difference was my better ability with the putter. On the greens, I took a total of 57 shots for the 36 holes; Phil took 65. In total, I one putted on 17 — nearly half the play-off holes — while Phil had only eight one-putt greens.

Other tournaments in which I enjoyed some exceptional putting were the 1968 Canadian Open and the 1969 World Match Play in London. In the latter, I sank putts of 20, 45 and 27 feet (6, 13.5 and 8 metres) in the last 10 holes to force a play-off to beat American Gene Littler.

It was nearly 10 years before I again experienced a great sequence of long putts. This was during the 1978 Air New Zealand Shell Open on the Titirangi Course in Auckland. Playing with Arnold Palmer and Peter Thomson before thousands of my own countrymen and women, I put the ball in the cup from all over the place. In round two where I scored 64, I recall putts of 20, 17 and 24 feet (6, 5 and 7 metres) dropping loudly, but sweetly into the cup. I also sank many 7 to 14 feet (2 to 4 metre) putts.

At a press conference Arnold Palmer said, "Bob is certainly still the best putter in the world after today's exhibition."

In 1983 at Tallahassee I holed from 10 feet (3 metres) on the 71st hole, 8 feet (2.5 metres) on the 72nd to go into a play-off where I made 50 feet (15.5 metres) on the first hole to seal victory.

To me, putting is the easiest part of the game, because there are fewer moving parts in the body in putting, and no physical strength is required. In theory a 10 year old child or an 80 year old should be able to putt as effectively as a tournament professional. There are, however, many variables which separate the good putter from the bad.

Next to the stroke itself, perhaps the most important consideration is an ability to *read* greens and to be able to judge the speed, the pace and the line of the putt. This can only be developed through experience and hours of practice under many different conditions. A good eye-hand co-ordination are also essential.

In my view, the most important facet of putting is having the right mental approach — confidence in your technique and ability. If you believe you can hole your putts, you may not hole every one but you will surprise your opponents by how many you do make. On the other hand, if you believe you are a bad putter who cannot get the ball into the hole, there is no way in the world that

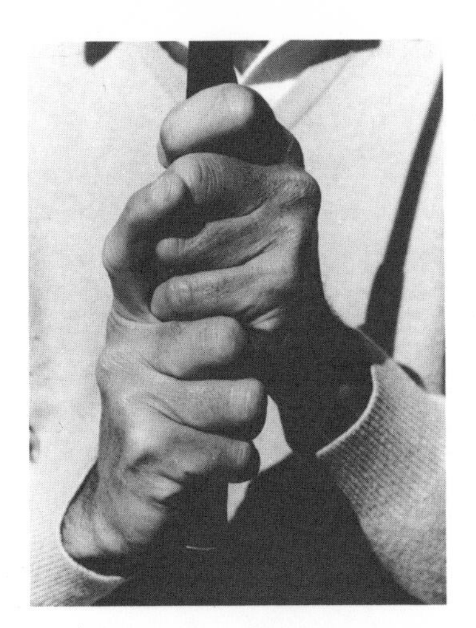

A My putting grip from the front showing the thumbs straight down the top of the shaft. There is a flat area on top of my grip to achieve this comfortable position. The back of the left hand faces towards the target area, and the back of the right hand faces directly away from the intended line.

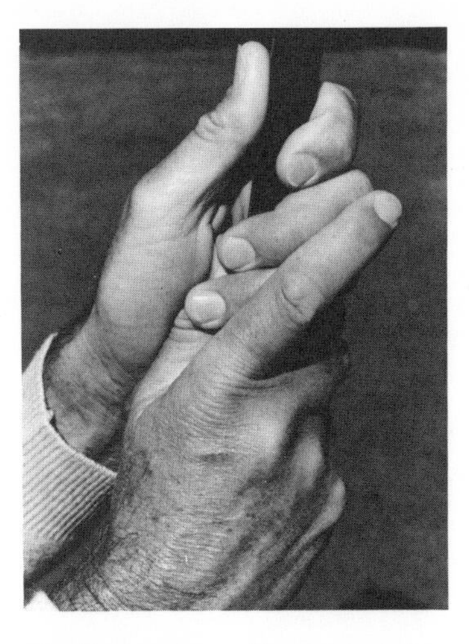

B The reverse overlap grip shows how the index finger of the right overlaps the second two fingers of the left hand.

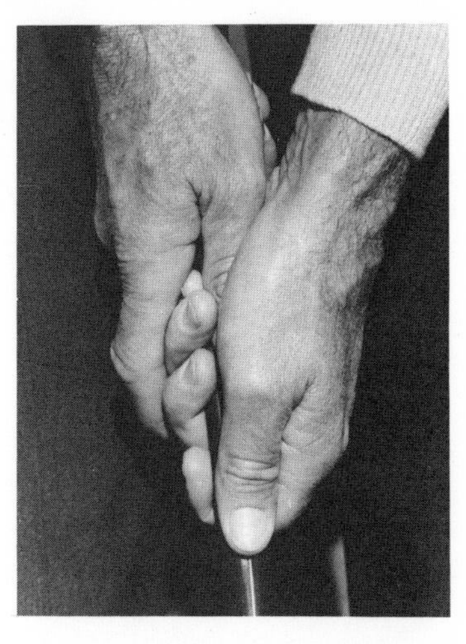

C From the back, all the fingers are close together on the grip except, of course, the index finger of the right hand. Having them close together improves the feel and allows them to work together as a single unit.

D In this picture with the Funk Setup Master my feet are about 14 inches (35 centimetres) apart. The head is directly over the ball; the hands are slightly ahead of the clubhead to help the ball to get a good roll.

E A rear view of my putting stance. The ball is about 10 inches (25 centimetres) from my feet, which places my eyes directly over the ball. The knees are comfortably flexed with no tension at all in any part of my body. There is a straight line up the shaft and forearms to my elbow. My hands are a comfortable distance from my thighs, giving freedom of movement.

The most important features are the square position of feet, knees, hips and shoulders, lined up perfectly with the intended line of the ball.

F Address position for the putter, without the Setup Master.

G The start of my takeaway or backswing with firm wrists. The only moving parts have been the arms and shoulders. Remember the pendulum action — back and through.

H Putting — completion of swing. Here, too, the only moving parts have been the arms and the shoulders. My head has moved only after the ball was on its way.

I Another shot of the takeaway showing the clubface still square to the target and slightly inside the intended line.

J After impact. The ball is just on its way, and my head has barely moved from the address. The clubface is square on line to the hole assisted by the pendulum action.

K The follow through is complete and the head can now turn so the eyes can follow the ball into the hole. The clubface has stayed on the line to the hole and is still almost square to that line.

you will ever get good results.

Technique is often said to be the key to success on the putting green, but I don't really regard it as vital for good results, because in my many years of travelling I have seen putts holed with all kinds of unusual techniques: some with open clubfaces, some coming across the ball, some coming inside it. The one thing they have in common is the player's ability to start the ball on the line required for the ball to fall into the hole.

The grip

The grip I have used throughout my career is a reverse overlap which positions the shaft more in the fingers of the right hand to give more feel. The thumbs of both hands are placed on top of the shaft, pointing towards the putter head as in Photographs A, B, and C. Another important feature of the grip is that the back of the right hand is facing directly towards the intended line of the ball, while the back of the left hand is facing directly away from the line of the ball. All the fingers are close together, particularly the index finger of the left hand.

The stance

I use a square stance, with the feet, hips and shoulders square with the intended line of the ball. I keep my eyes directly over the ball. You can check this for yourself by using the putter as a plumb-bob from between your eyes. This is a very comfortable position, with the weight evenly distributed between the left and right feet and between the heels and toes.

The stroke

The type of stroke I use is rather like a pendulum. The fulcrum of the pendulum is my head; the arms and club are the extension. This makes my wrists lock. The stroke is basically an arm and shoulder movement beginning with address or set-up, the takeaway and follow through. An important feature is that the follow through should be as long as or longer than the backswing or takeaway. Naturally, the shorter the putt the shorter the pendulum, and the longer the putt the longer the pendulum.

In the backswing, the club comes back slightly inside the line, due to the angle of the putter shaft. The head must remain quite still until the ball is on its way. Not until completion of the forward movement of the club should the head come up to observe the ball running, hopefully, into the hole.

Knowing how to read greens is the real stroke-saver, though, and learning all you can about this can mean the difference between winning big and not making it at all. Travelling throughout the world learning about different types of greens during various seasons has helped me immeasurably. I believe it is the main reason for my good putting. If you have to stick to just one or two courses, don't worry. Regardless of the grass variety — bluegrass, Bermuda, rye, bent or any of the many new combinations, you can adjust quickly as long as you work out the direction of the grain, and notice and allow for any break or borrow between ball and cup, and determine whether the surface putts fast or slow.

Grass on the greens, especially Bermuda and the coarser varieties, grows in a particular direction; usually, though not always, it is towards the sun and the sea, and away from mountains. Knowing this can help to make you aware of some of the hidden tricks that a strange course may throw at you. You should always check the lie of the grass. The best way to do this is to read it by its shine. If the grass is light coloured, you are looking with the grain; if it is a deep shade of green, you are going into or against the grain. If you cannot make up your mind about the grass, check the hole itself. You can easily see the way the grain is growing. The worn side of the cup will indicate the grain going towards that side. This is what the touring professional is checking when he is seen peering intently into the cavity.

The way some greens are cut also influences the roll of the ball. At the Augusta National course in Georgia, the site of the famed Masters Tournament, the greens are cut up and down and also crossways. This makes it extremely difficult to detect any grain, or its direction, so you don't have to worry about it except in the immediate vicinity of the hole, where you can spot the direction by looking into the cup and checking the grain above the dirt line.

On greens that are cut in two directions only, a definite nap is produced. This is much easier to detect and allow for as you putt.

Going with the grain, the putt will be stroked much more easily than when you have to hit into it. Putting across grain, you should adjust your stroke depending on the length of the putt and the strength of the grain. The grain will have little effect on the ball as it leaves the putter blade, travelling at maximum speed, but when the ball begins to slow down, the green pulls it in the direction of the grain. A putt that is timidly hit may twist crazily at the hole.

On most putts, I prefer to lag the ball. I feel that a dying putt has much more chance of dropping in the hole than a putt that is running fast for the hole to just catch the lip. The dying putt will go in every time; the other will hit the rim, spin around and stay out. I hit my putts much more softly than most other tournament golfers do, even the short ones. I like to just trickle the ball into the hole. Coarse, grainy Bermuda grass greens need firmer strokes, but I am definitely not a charge putter.

The way you putt is a matter of individual taste, and I won't insist that my way is right. But it is true that the weekend golfer whose skills are rusted by inactivity would be better using the lag putting technique than charging the ball. Leave the charging putt for those who feel they can always hole the one coming back. If you are totally confident in your putting, bang it, under the never up, never in philosophy. If not, lag it up and let it die in the hole.

Chapter Eleven

Weather conditions

EVERY golfer has good days, and bad ones too. With these changing moods, often brought about because of the weather, it is necessary to adapt your game so you can play as well as possible.

In good weather, with the sun shining, no more than a whisper of wind, and the rain miles away, I enjoy my golf much better than when the winds are strong and the rain is falling.

Sometimes you do have to use a low shot. You may have to hit into the wind and keep your ball low to avoid tree branches or other obstacles. I play this kind of shot with the ball lying back towards my left foot. This makes certain that my hands keep moving well in front of the clubhead. Hitting the ball more on the downswing will produce a shot with a much lower path. This works whether your swing is upright or flat.

In the United States, wind is not such a big problem as it is in New Zealand or on the famous seaside courses of Great Britain, where so many important championships are played. But wind on any course in any country will play havoc with players' attitudes and, of course, with their scores. There is some consolation in the fact that it is the same for everyone. If you are scoring badly in bad weather there are lots of others who are also having trouble with the conditions.

There are some specific ways of handling the wind.

Hitting into the wind

The wind that comes directly at you will make the ball do strange things, emphasising even a very small mistake you might have made in hitting the ball. To avoid problems I suggest that when playing this shot you should firm up everything and concentrate on a shorter backswing. Your footwork will be more secure and you should hit the ball with a crispness you'll enjoy. When hitting an approach into the green with the wind at your face, hit the ball straight at the pin. With normal backspin on the ball intensified by the wind, you can be certain that the ball is going to hit into the surface, dance momentarily and then settle.

Downwind floaters

Approach shots with the wind at your back can often be tougher and more wearing than those you have to hit into the wind. There is none of the helpful spin that a headwind can give to the ball. Carried aloft by the wind the ball floats longer and tends to be uncontrollable which is, of course, frustrating. Always allow for maximum roll. It is helpful to use a more lofted club than normal. During execution try to resist the temptation to rush the shot and possibly come off the ball.

Crosswind shots

Another wind that causes problems to all of us blows across the fairways. The crosswind can blow from left to right, or right to left, or it can be part of a downwind or a headwind. Regardless of its type, play with it. Do not try to hold the ball into it. It

No one likes playing golf in the wet, least of all me. But as a long-time professional I must go where the tournaments take me, irrespective of the weather. Here I am in Auckland, New Zealand, not looking at all happy but well equipped for the weather nevertheless. My caddy is Michael Glading, son of the former New Zealand Open champion Bob Glading. *Auckland Star*

would be silly to try to hook a ball into a wind that is blowing from one side to another. Leave those fancy shots to the pros. In the same way, if the wind is coming from in front or from behind at an oblique angle, compensate by playing the shot to bring the ball into the target area at its own speed. Never try to fight it.

Rain

Wind can cause problems, but golf in the rain is an uncomfortable experience. If the wind is blowing as well, things can be even more difficult.

I think that with the right approach, you can score well in the rain. If you go out determined to make the most of the conditions you will be at peace with yourself and have a chance of playing well.

When playing in the rain keep *yourself* as dry as possible and also make sure your clubs are kept dry. Plenty of wet weather equipment is available; it weighs very little and can be easily packed into your golf bag. Wear rubber golf shoes or good quality leather shoes with spikes to give you a firm footing. Many amateur golfers allow their spikes to wear down, and when bad weather strikes their footwear is unsuitable for the conditions. Footwear is expensive but do try to have two pairs of shoes and change them daily.

Keep your hands and the grips on your clubs dry so there is no slipping when making shots; also keep the clubface dry. If water fills the scored lines that run across the blade, the ball will fly off with no spin and no control. Under the Rules of Golf, you are allowed to wipe the clubface before each shot. It is a good idea to spend a little time doing this. Because there will be some moisture left on the clubhead, the ball will still tend to fly, so you should allow for some extra run. Play for the front of the green if the pin is, say, 20 or 30 feet (6 or 9 metres) into the cut area. *A firm stance* is important for confident shot making. In wet weather the ground often becomes slippery on top and unless your spikes are good and you have set yourself up well, you can slide when you play your shot. When the ground is slippery it is advisable to widen your stance and shorten your backswing.

If the fairways are soft from the rain the risk of the ball bouncing into the rough is eliminated, so you can play a bolder stroke with possible dividends. If the greens are soaked you will be able to hit the ball right up to the hole, knowing that it will sit down well.

One characteristic of wet weather golf is that though the greens may be very wet, they can also be very fast. A little water, not enough for a good soaking, and they will maintain their slickness. Greens that have been hard and fast before the rain can retain that slickness for some time, so take care as you line up those always vital putts.

At times greens become very heavy. You can usually identify a heavy green by looking for surface water, or water that squelches up when you walk onto the putting surface. Putt boldly on heavy greens. The ball will not break as much as under dry conditions, so you can hit it more firmly and straighter for the hole than you would on a dry green.

I don't think most golfers think enough about the rules of the game, especially the relief allowable in wet weather.

If you are going to play in the wet, spend a few minutes reading the Casual Water rule. Casual water is defined as "... any temporary accumulation of water which is visible before or after the player takes his/her stance and which is not a hazard of itself or is not in a water hazard." Snow and ice are also casual water unless otherwise determined by Local Rules. In New Zealand where most club golf is played in the winter, and in some areas in snow and ice, a good knowledge of the rules can be rewarding.

The rules also cover putting conditions: "... on the putting green, or if such conditions intervene between a ball lying on the green and the hole, the player may lift the ball and place it without penalty in the nearest position to where it lay which affords maximum relief from these conditions, but not nearer the hole."

Cold days

Often people have said to me, "It must be great always following the sun." Much though I enjoy warm weather, the professional life is not always like that.

Professional golfers have no control over the weather, and if we are to pay the bills we have got to tee it up in all kinds of conditions — sunshine, wind, rain, oppressive humidity or bitter cold. Each condition has to be handled in a different way. When it is cold you have to stay warm but retain freedom of movement. This means no bulky sweaters or jackets; instead, we have adopted thermal underwear from the skiers. A hat, a woollen, long-sleeved shirt and a lightweight sweater or windbreaker are usually enough to keep the cold out. Heavy winter gloves or mittens lined with wool are essential to keep the hands warm between shots so you do not lose the feel of the clubs.

Then there is your *golf ball*. Yes, a ball that is warm does go further than one that is cold, so if you have to play in wintry conditions keep a spare ball or two in your pockets, warmed up ready for action.

Hot days

Hot days are frequent in the United States and also Down Under, especially when the professionals are playing their major events. Selection of clothing for these conditions is every bit as important as when playing in the cold. For example, light coloured slacks and short sleeved shirts will not attract the heat as much as dark clothing. Some form of headgear is advisable for protection. Because the hands and arms will perspire, dry towels should be taken along as well as some spare golf gloves. Drink plenty of water to counter dehydration.

When the air is humid, personal comfort may be asking too much. We have to accept such conditions, but I do suggest that you slow the pace a little so you do not become exhausted. Also try to stay out of the sun as much as possible. Use the shade of the trees between shots or when waiting to play.

High altitudes

Most golfers will enjoy playing at least one round where the air is thin because at high altitudes well hit shots will travel further than they do at or close to sea level. You can get an extra 15 to 25 yards (15 to 20 metres) with your driver.

But high conditions play havoc with club selection for approaches to the green. Plan your approach shots and use a more lofted club than you would play for a similar distance shot at home and you will soon adjust to the conditions.

Chapter Twelve

"Different" shots

THE left hander will not often feel handicapped because of the way he or she has to stand to the ball. Occasionally a hole will dogleg in the wrong direction for us, and the shot that would put us into proper position will be the one shot that does not produce any distance at all. Otherwise, the golf courses are true tests that continually challenge the player from tee to green. It pays to plan how to attack each hole well in advance.

But even the best laid plans go astray and when you find yourself off the track and in trouble, you need to know how to keep calm and come up with the proper shot.

If you want to reach a high standard and stay there, you need to develop a repeating swing with a good feel that will stand up under the pressure of play. If the swing goes off slightly, the ball's line should not be affected.

Around this principle most touring professionals have devised their way of manoeuvring or working the ball. Because they come into the ball almost the same way every time, they consistently hit the straight ball.

The hook and the fade

Here's how the professionals do it. First, to hook the ball — that is, draw it from left to right, close your stance by pulling the left foot back from the line of flight, and swing inside out. Work the club from inside the line, letting the clubhead catch up with the hands. Occasionally, I also close the clubface slightly and roll my wrists after impact to accentuate the bend I want to put on the ball.

If I want to fade, I take the club absolutely straight from the ball and return it on the outside of the line of flight, concentrating on cutting across the ball without using too much left hand in the shot, all from an open stance.

For the slice, keep the hands ahead of the clubhead with an open face.

Experiment with your grip by moving the hands into the weak position, more to your right and on top of the shaft to help produce a fade, or into the strong position by moving both hands more to the left, under the shaft to obtain a hook.

You may not have found it easy to develop a good grip for your straight shots, so once you have it correctly aligned and perfectly atuned leave it alone. To make the ball move to the right or left, change only your stance or swing plane.

Next time you are on the practice area, you can help yourself to understand how to hit them straight if you spend some time deliberately making the ball bend.

Hilly lies

Sometimes the ups and downs of the weather are easier to contend with than the ups and downs of golf course fairways, even though those hilly lies do make the game more interesting.

Uphill, sidehill and downhill shots can play havoc with your score, especially if you are faced with a lot of them.

Most of the world's great courses feature

A The hook or draw: I am about to play the shot which is a left to right action around the tree directly in front of me. My stance is closed, with the left foot back from the line of flight.

B The fade: my stance is open for this shot, which is also known as a slice. The ball is played from right to left.

C For the downhill lie, the ball is positioned back in the stance, with the weight on the front or, in my case, the right foot. This allows the club arc to travel along the line of the slope.

D Going uphill means you have to play the ball forward off the right heel, with the weight more on the inside of the left foot at address to allow the club arc to travel with the slope.

undulating fairways, so everyone runs into this problem. The golfer who knows how to play these shots will be at home anywhere.

The toughest of these situations is the downhill shot, especially if length is also required. Be sure to keep the weight on the right foot so the arc stays with the contour of the ground. This will cause the ball to be played a bit left of centre because the club will contact it first. Take the club back fairly normally, unless the contour dictates otherwise. The swing into the ball should be smooth and uninterrupted, with the clubhead following the ground's contour.

Move the clubhead through the ball, without lifting or raising the body at impact. The hands generally precede the clubhead. This shot should produce roll, so the club selected might be one less than normal. The chief fault is hitting behind the ball. Maintain balance and a steady head position, hit through the ball rhythmically, and another of golf's rewarding shots will be yours.

Going uphill requires you to play the ball up forward. Gravity pull will force your weight to move back to your left side, so make certain your knee does not buckle further to the left. Keep your weight on the inside of the left foot, and restrict the backswing so you do not sway on your way back, and open your stance a little. The backswing is otherwise normal with regard to plane, so return to the ball as with other good shots. Change your hand position slightly if you wish to keep the ball low (move them ahead of the blade) or high (keep them slightly behind the blade). This shot will cause the ball to travel in a higher trajectory and not as far, so use a club a little longer than you would normally. Hitting uphill is exactly opposite to hitting downhill.

Playing sidehill lies can be perplexing. If the ball is lower than the feet it is particularly difficult. The tendency is to push or slice the ball. Allow for this by moving your stance to the right as though you were aiming for a spot to the right of the green. At address you will stand closer to the ball. Use a longer club. Most importantly, concentrate on good balance, keeping most of your weight on your heels throughout the swing. At execution the ball should drift to the left and if your club selection has been good, the shot should take you onto the putting surface.

When the ball is higher than your feet, the swing flattens; you are forced to stand a little further from the ball, and a hook is generally the result. Change your stance so you are aiming to the left of the green. Choke up on the club and play the ball a bit left of centre — towards the toes. Again, good balance is essential with the weight more towards the toes.

If you are a left hander and your tee shot is destined to go off the fairway, it is better if it stays to the left. Then, unless your error was very bad, you would at least be standing on or near the fairway and away from problems such as trees and bushes. It is bad enough to have your ball settled down in the rough, without having to try to fit your body comfortably into a space that is too small before you can play a shot. If the ball is in thick grass, forget the idea of going for distance; don't even consider using a wood or long iron. Instead, be satisfied with positioning your next shot for a better approach to the green.

The problem here is two-fold. You have to take the club into the air rather abruptly on the backswing so it does not snarl in the grass; you must also bring the clubface down sharply on the ball so it will rise quickly without danger of burrowing in deeper. The weight for this type of shot is either evenly distributed or in towards the heels slightly to offset any body motion towards the ball. A forward tilt of the body pushes the blade outside the line and encourages an occasional hit on the hosel of the club. This sends your ball sharply off to the left, almost laterally away from your target. The approach shot from the rough requires a smooth, even tempo.

At times when the grass is thin and not

too resistant, you might get away with using a wood. This club has a long shaft and can build up clubhead speed easily; the head can cut through the grass and there is enough weight and loft to ride through the grass and get into the ball without strain.

From about 170 yards (155 metres) out, play this shot as much like a fairway shot as you can, with the same body turn, weight shift and follow through.

The circumstances of the lie and general conditions of play, as well as what's at stake, must, of course, be considered. But normally the ball will not travel as high as the same shot from the fairway, and it will roll much further.

It is difficult to control a shot from the rough, but it is part of the game, so don't feel too badly when the ball bounces into the heavier grass.

In the rough

Playing a shot from the rough within 60 yards (55 metres) of the green can be more difficult. The distance requires a full shot, but you cannot be certain of what lies under the ball and you can never be sure how the ball or the club will react. It is wiser to use a No. 9 iron rather than the wedge, which with its heavy flange might bounce off the ground or off the packed, thick grass and skull the ball. The sharper leading edge of the No. 9 iron is more suited to handle this problem and the results can be much more consistently judged.

If the grass is so thick that it hides a good portion of the ball, make sure you first identify the ball as yours before you hit. It is legal to do so. Playing the wrong ball can cost you the hole in match-play or two strokes in stroke play.

And that clearly would be *rough*!

Chapter Thirteen

Highs, lows and great moments

Highs and lows

UNLESS a professional is winning several major events each year, the media tend to write them off as over the hill.

And as one gets older, victories, especially in golf, do in fact become fewer, so the press cuttings become less favourable. I am one of those golfers who doesn't get upset by media comment, although I do read everything written about the events I play in. Now, as I approach the age of 50 I look forward to joining the United States Seniors' tour. A whole new career is opening up for me.

Fortunately, I keep very good health and with my game continuing to stand up to the rigour of year-round tournament play, hopefully I'll still be swinging my clubs well in another decade. Naturally, I expect fewer tournament victories because players who are younger than me will eventually turn 50 and join me on the seniors' circuit.

Highs

As I stand on the threshold of 50 and look back on 25 years as a professional golfer, I have many memories: of my 1963 win in the Houston Classic, a key factor in winning the British Open that same year. It gave me confidence in myself and reinforced my view that continuous tournament play in America was sharpening my game, that helped me to beat Phil Rodgers in that British Open play-off at Royal Lytham and St Anne's.

Yes, the 1963 British Open has been the highlight of my career. I believe that any young golfer embarking on a career as a tournament player should aim to win a major championship such as the British Open, the United States Open, the United States PGA and the United States Masters. I won only one of those events, but I had a second in the United States PGA, just one shot behind the winner and was third on two occasions in the United States Open. But the Masters at Augusta was not one of my better events, my best finish being 15th.

Having won one major, I would have liked to win a second, but I doubt that will ever happen. I do not feel the British Open was a one-off situation and would not like to think it was considered a fluke — rather a great achievement.

Naturally, I have great pride in the British Open title and it is nice to be remembered as a former Open Champion. Indeed, throughout my playing days I have enjoyed considerable success in the United Kingdom and have generally found the galleries to be most appreciative of good play and they have an excellent understanding of the game.

I have won several other majors in Britain including the 1969 World Match play and back to back victories in 1972 with the John Player Classic and the Dunlop Masters titles.

Winning in one's own country is always satisfying. Victories in New Zealand have been perhaps even more important to me than winning in other countries, because they have kept my name in front of the public and enabled me to retain contracts

A mother's pride — Bob and his mother Phyllis after he had won the 1954 New Zealand Open as an eighteen-year-old amateur.

with sporting goods manufacturers. I have won numerous New Zealand Open titles and PGA championships, including the 1978 Air New Zealand Shell Open.

Following that win, I continued to play well from 1978 to 1983, when the highlights were another New Zealand title, the PGA in 1980 and the 1983 Tallahassee Open.

Golf has been good to me and it has given me great satisfaction and enjoyment.

Lows

There is a period in any career when sportspeople experience periods of despair.

My first real low was in 1966, when there was a downturn in my form following an important victory just a year earlier in the Tucson Open. My problem was in my tee shots. Bob Toski put me right. (See Chapter 1.)

Three years later I dipped again. 1970 and 1971 were real lows, so much so that I then decided to move off the United States tour.

Through 1975, 1976 and 1977 my game also went through a down period. Victories eluded me although I continued to make enough money to take care of my family.

Great moments

I'm lucky to have Jim Wallace as a co-author. Not only has he put a lot of time and expertise into this book but he's a personal friend and as a journalist has reported on hundreds of golf tournaments, including many of my own. This is clear in the rest of this chapter which, in all modesty, I could never have written for myself.

New Zealand Open 1954

In 1978 after Bob Charles had beaten a very strong field to win the Air New Zealand Shell Open on the Titirangi course in New Zealand, Arnold Palmer called him "the best putter in the world".

Charles had been a tournament winner in many parts of the world over a long period, and some of those victories were clearly due to superb displays of putting supported by a good all-round game.

In 1954 Charles, then only 18 years old and an amateur, stunned the golfing fraternity of Australia and New Zealand by winning his country's national open championship. It was a win that had golfers buzzing with excitement. It also caught the imagination of all New Zealanders with an interest in sport. His victory in that Open Championship by two shots from Bruce Crampton of Australia, who later became a major success in the United States, and four ahead of title-holder Peter Thomson, now a regular competitor on the United States Seniors' tour, was the sort of stuff to make sporting page headlines.

Terry McLean, one of New Zealand's best known sports writers eulogised Charles: "King Charles has taken over the throne of Peter the Great; [Peter Thomson had won the New Zealand Open in 1950, 1951, 1953 and 1955 — and later in 1959, 1960, 1961, 1965 and 1971.]

"The actual deposing of royalty always arouses a certain feeling of melancholy; but this is, I think, an occasion when we might all imagine ourselves to be peers and peeresses standing in the galleries and raising the cry, at a given signal, 'Long live the King! Long live the King!'

"Amid scenes of great emotion Charles was crowned King. His score of 280 equalled Peter Thomson's record at Shirley in 1950; he had the better, by two strokes, of another young, though slightly more solid, pretender in Bruce Crampton, the Sydney assistant professional, who had played for Australia as an amateur and who, in the opinion of Norman Von Nida, is the next Australian to beat the world.

"He had the better of Thomson by four strokes; and though it was only his second attempt at the Open, though his experience in competition is practically nil, though he is 18, and though he is a member of the Lost Tribe of Left-handers, he had the beating of the best other New Zealander, D. L. (Tim) Woon, by no fewer than six strokes.

"As the tournament wandered on to a triumphant finish, Crampton and Woon won their separate glories, Crampton by winning the professional championship and Woon by a dazzlingly high-powered exhibiton in the Amateur.

"King Charles he became, and though he may never again perform such a deed, though his future may be troubled by drives that whistle over the fence and putts that slide by the hole, King Charles he will always remain.

"There has never before been a performance like this in New Zealand golf. I seriously suggest that it compares well if on a more modest scale, with the epochal achievement of Francis Ouimet in beating Harry Vardon and Ted Ray in 1913, and with the feat of Bobby Locke in winning the South African Open at the age of 18 — though they, bless them, weren't left-handers!"

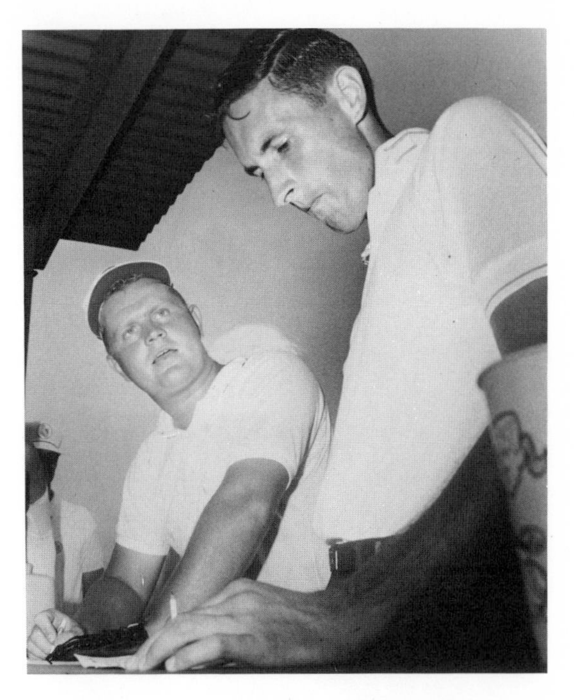

Charles' first big win in the USA — checking his card alongside Jack Nicklaus after winning the 1963 Houston Classic.

In 1954 *The Standard*, then the official New Zealand Labour Party weekly newspaper, devoted considerable space to Charles' victory:

"For his own welfare and in the interests of New Zealand golf, the boy wonder Bob Charles must be sent overseas, preferably to the United States at the earliest opportunity. . . . Charles is such a wonderful prospect that it would be sheer tragedy to keep him within the confines of our own shores. Charles is talent with a capital 'T'. There is no saying what heights he would scale with tough, testing overseas experience under his belt. . . . Charles is already a champion golfer by New Zealand standards.

"But he also has that extra something which is not usually associated with even top flight New Zealand golfers.

"That extra something is intense concentration, so intense in fact that he is almost to the point of being taciturn when playing,

Taking a break from the strain of the US tour: here Bob Charles tries his hand at baseball with his son David.

The 1954 New Zealand Open scoreboard
(Each professional marked with an asterisk)

Total	Name	Scores
280	R. J. Charles (Masterton)	69, 72, 68, 71
282	*B. Crampton (Beverley Park, NSW)	74, 72, 68, 68
284	*P. W. Thomson (Victoria, Australia)	71, 71, 73, 69
286	D. L. Woon (Hamilton)	71, 73, 74, 68
288	*E. A. Southerden (Napier)	74, 77, 71, 66
	*A. E. Guy (unattached)	75, 69, 73, 71
	W. G. Horne (Wellington)	74, 74, 70, 70
	*F. X. Buckler (unattached)	76, 69, 71, 72
289	*J. A. Paterson (Tauranga)	72, 73, 74, 70

though off the links he is a quiet, likeable youth."

The Standard summed up: "At last New Zealand golf has the youngster it's been hoping for since the immediate post war years. And now that it's got him it must look after him."

One so young who had toppled "giants" and "kings" could have been excused for becoming over excited at the prize-giving and making rash predictions about his future. But he thanked his opponents for their competition, his parents for their support and encouragement, and the host club for making the 1954 Open a fine event.

He then went back to the bank in Masterton and continued his career in commerce, a career which two years later took him to Christchurch. This city and golfing friends he made there were to have a significant influence on his game.

His membership of the Christchurch Golf Club in Shirley put him alongside another fine sportsman, Ian Cromb, who played to a handicap of one. Cromb had walked the Heretaunga course in 1954 watching almost every shot played by the left hander on his way to the Open title. He was convinced that Charles should be encouraged to develop a game in which he displayed a maturity and understanding far beyond the abilities of many golfers twice his age and experience.

Houston Classic 1963

American professionals had become accustomed to playing against overseas players in their circuit events and, therefore, it was no surprise when Charles appeared in the United States early in 1963 to play his first full tour of the United States circuit, although he had played five events in 1962.

His early tournaments at Phoenix (where he had played in 1958 during his US/UK tour with Ian Cromb as an amateur); at Tuscon in New Orleans, the Pensacola and the famed Masters at Augusta saw him collect enough money to pay expenses which were not inconsiderable as the New Zealander, recently married, was touring with his wife Verity.

Perhaps the presence and influence of Verity gave him the determination to show the United States professionals that this left-handed New Zealander was a golfer of talent and determination.

Encouraged by winnings of $1100 in the Masters; $1760 at Greater Greensboro, and more in the New Orleans open where he finished fourth, he arrived in Houston feeling that his game was reaching a peak. It was.

"I started with a 67 — three under par," said Charles, "and found myself trailing the leader, Tommy Aaron, by three shots. I did even better on day two; I shot 66 and went into the lead. It was a good feeling, though I was nervous. And I knew the pressure would be on over the following two days.

"Luckily my game was good enough. Another 66 in round three, then 69 on the last day gave me a 72-hole tournament record total of 268. I also beat Fred Hawkins by one shot. It was a good win.

"I was elated; I was on cloud nine, $10,000 as well. It was hard to believe . . . a great thrill and the incentive needed to go on to greater things."

Golf writers and commentators covering the event were interested in how Charles managed to play the game so well from the other side of the ball.

"I'm a natural left-hander at two handed sports like golf, baseball and cricket, and right-handed at tennis and squash. I started playing golf when very young. My parents were good at the game and they are left handers"

The Los Angeles Times: "Bob Charles, a lanky New Zealander, has 10,000 reasons, and they're all dollars, why golf is not strictly a right-hander's game. Charles the first southpaw ever to win a Professional Golf Association tournament took the $10,000 first prize yesterday in the Houston Classic. The splintery 27 year old with an accent right out of one of those old British movies seen frequently on television, took the lead in the second round and held off a strong finish by Fred Hawkins of El Paso, Texas to win by a stroke.

"Charles' 12 under par score of 67-66-66-69 — 268 broke the Classic's 72 hole record of 273 set by Cary Middlecoff in 1955."

New York, *The Post:* "A new day is coming for the natural left-handed golfer, hurried a bit perhaps by the $10,000 triumph in the Houston Classic by R. J. Charles of New Zealand."

About five per cent of the American golf population are left-handers (about 250,000) but the range of golf clubs available is not as great as the equipment for the right-handed player.

Herman Harron, the national PGA senior

champion would still convert a left-hander to the right side because the equipment is so superior.

"Let 'em play left-handed," said Gus Popp, a New York club professional, "if they're playing just for fun. But if it's for a career, I'd tell 'em to play right-handed."

New York Herald Tribune: "Between Billie Sol Estes, with his fertilizer, and the National League Umpires with their new version of the balk rule, this spring in Texas has been a rough deal all round.

"The worst came to pass in a $50,000 clambake called the Houston Classic, an annual fiesta dedicated to the glory and greed of that god-like creature the lone star golfer.

"By sacred tradition, if not State Law, this is a private bash where carpet-baggers are tolerated only on condition that they leave the prize money to some deserving son of the purple plains like Byron Nelson, Ben Hogan or Jimmy Demaret.

"Well, Texans, it must have been something to behold when a tall, skinny stranger who looks like Charles de Gaulle but calls himself Bob Charles went busting round with scores of 67-66-66-69 — 268 smashing the tournament record by five strokes and making off with $10,000.

"Not only is Charles a non-Texan, he's a non-Texan from a place called New Zealand, which is a heck of a piece beyond the Pecos and on top of that he's left-handed.

"It was by all odds, the most horrid calamity since the Alamo."

British Open 1963

The British Press has never lacked imagination.

"Charles the First!"; "It's Run-away Charles"; "Putt Goes Charles — and Phut Goes Rodgers". These headlines were carried by the British Press on a July day in 1963 after Bob Charles won the world's most prestigious golf championship, the British Open, on the Royal Lytham and St Anne's course on the bleak Lancashire Coast.

In a country where people will bet on anything, Bob Charles was not in the running. Some bookmakers must have been sorry when Charles took the title and they had to pay out to his supporters.

Charles went into the Open full of confidence; his victory at Houston three months earlier had convinced him that he had both the game and the temperament for the big time.

"Looking back," said Charles, "I didn't have any real ideas about winning the Open, though since Houston I had been building my game for this tournament."

A 67 in practice was followed by a first round of 68 which had Charles just one stroke behind the man of the moment, Peter Thomson of Australia, and American Phil Rodgers. Driving badly twice — at the third and the 15th — in the second round, he took a pair of sixes and carded a two over par 72 which left him five behind Rodgers, four behind Thomson and two behind Jack Nicklaus who, as expected, had made a forward move.

"The pressure was really on as we went into round three," said Charles, "with placings changing dramatically. I had a 66 which broke the course record, and went to a one stroke lead on 206 over Thomson, with Nicklaus and Rodgers two away on 208.

"Thomson faded in the final round but Nicklaus was a threat. He held a one stroke lead with 11 holes left to play. But I caught him and went to a one stroke lead after the 12th. Nicklaus was playing ahead of Phil and me. He went to pieces on the last two holes, carding bogey fives. Phil and I were really under pressure. We had no time to relax, even for a moment. With regulation fours on the 71st and 72nd holes, we tied up the Open and went home knowing that tomorrow we faced 36 holes to decide the outcome of the 1963 British Open.

"Those two rounds became a test of endurance as well as a test of golf. I think

An historic picture. My wife Verity and myself with the 1963 British Open trophy. I was the first left-hander to win the British Open — and so far I'm still the only one.

one round of 18 holes would have been more than enough, but the rules had to be obeyed and we had to play 36.

"After the first 18 holes I had a three stroke advantage over Rodgers. I was round in 69, including only 26 putts. No fewer than 11 of these were single putted greens.

"I won strokes on the first two holes after lunch and led by five. Then, unaccountably, I pulled my tee shot onto the railway line, suffered a two stroke penalty and saw Rodgers have two threes to my two fours and reduce the lee-way to one stroke with 12 left to play. He shanked a bunker explosion on the seventh and I moved to two up coming to the eighth — the hole that sealed the championship.

"I concentrated on getting my pars from the ninth to the end of the round. I knew that would give me the championship.

"I was right and I finally won by eight strokes.

"I was on cloud nine as the media flocked around me. Suddenly everyone wanted to talk to the New Zealander who hit the ball from the wrong side."

Charles' victory was headlined in the mass circulation Sunday papers, *The Sunday Express, News of the World, The Guardian, The People* and other major newspapers. *News of the World's* Edgar Turner said Charles won with "some of the most amazing putting ever seen". In the same newspaper, Henry Cotton wrote that Charles "gave an exhibition of brilliant putting such as has probably never been seen in an important championship." Cotton went on to say that not even Bobby

Locke, Peter Thomson, Walter Hagen, Arnold Palmer, or Bobby Jones had ever putted better. "Time after time, the ball rolled gently into the tin from all lengths as though pulled by an invisible thread."

Sydney Spicer in *The Sunday Express* said Charles won "with a short game of sustained and almost uncanny brilliance".

The People described Charles as "Golf's Thin Man" and said his golf could be summed up in one word — "ruthless".

Pat Ward-Thomas, of *The Guardian* wrote: "No left-handed golfer in the history of the game has achieved eminence in any way comparable to that of Charles, whose position now is quite unique. All over the world when children grasp the club the wrong way round, parents henceforth may think again before insisting on the change. Left-handers are common in other games, but in golf they are rare birds who, with notable exceptions like P. B. Lucas, look strange and often ungainly. . . .

"Charles, without question is one of the world's finest putters, and this alone is proof of his competitive quality. Under the acute and mounting pressure of the last round his wonderfully true, firm and deliberate strokes never faltered. He gave an exhibition of putting which has rarely been surpassed; it tortured and destroyed Rodgers with a merciless finality which was almost inhuman. . . .

"Rodgers was unfortunate to be three strokes behind at lunch for Charles was down in a single putt no less than eleven times. This revealed, with some truth, that his golf through the green was less accurate than that of Rodgers. Palmer had said the previous evening that if Rodgers started putting well he would win. As it happened he did not, and when erring tee shots cost two more faults in the early afternoon all seemed over."

After the play-off, Leonard Crawley, a noted British golf writer, who first met Charles at the 1960 World Amateur teams' event at Merion, Philadelphia, felt the New Zealander would not survive in the professional game. He said this even after Charles turned professional: "We all knew him to be a good putter but when I heard that he was to turn professional I was surprised for I did not consider he had anything like the power to survive in world-class golf.

"He is, I submit, one of the few who have increased their natural speed of hand and gained length. I remember Henry Cotton telling me in the thirties, 'You have either got speed of hand or you have not. You cannot learn and you cannot teach it,' and he added: 'If I could learn how to teach it I would sit in a window in Picadilly and sell it. And what a fortune I should make!'

"That was a profound observation. Charles is a tall thin fellow and like other left-handed players, P. B. Lucas excepted, he is not easy to watch. There is something wooden about his swing but he has learned to make the ball travel.

"He is a marvellous putter with a complementary short game. He putts from a rocklike stance without even the movement of his dark eyebrows.

"On the course he gives the impression of being a grim customer and perhaps he is, but that is the way to win at this fierce game today."

The 1963 British Open scoreboard

277	Bob Charles (New Zealand)	68, 72, 66, 71
277	Phil Rodgers (United States)	67, 68, 73, 69

Play-off: Charles 69, 71 — 140;
Rodgers 72, 76 — 148

278	Jack Nicklaus (United States)	71, 67, 70, 70
283	Kel Nagle (Australia)	69, 70, 73, 71
285	Peter Thomson (Australia)	67, 69, 71, 78
286	Christy O'Connor (Ireland)	74, 68, 76, 68

Bob Charles' record in the British Open Championship

1962	5th
1963	1st
1964	17th =
1965	Missed the Cut
1966	37th =
1967	Missed the Cut
1968	2nd =
1969	2nd
1970	13th =
1971	18th =
1972	15th =
1973	7th =
1974	Missed the Cut
1975	12th =
1976	Missed the Cut
1977	43rd =
1978	48th =
1979	10th =
1980	60th =
1981	35th =
1982	Missed the Cut
1983	Did not Play
1984	47th = Was the oldest player to complete the four rounds.

Canadian Open 1968

After the excitement of 1963, Charles built on his game through the mid 1960s, picking up victories in the 1964 CBS four ball match play classic with Australian Bruce Devlin, the 1965 Tuscon Open, the 1967 Atlanta Classic. Then came 1968, which was to prove to be a busy and successful 12 months.

A highlight was his second equal placing with Jack Nicklaus in the British Open at Canoustie. He was also runner-up with Arnold Palmer in the United States PGA. But the crowning glory was the Canadian Open title and a cheque for $25,000.

About 20,000 spectators were on the course at St George's Golf Club, Toronto to see Charles hold off a group of 20, all within four strokes of each other in what was described as the tightest final round in the history of the coveted Canadian Open.

In a head to head tussle through the final round with Jack Nicklaus, the left hander was master on the greens. Charles held a one shot advantage at the last hole and he shut out the star American when he put a seven iron approach shot only nine inches (23 centimetres) from the pin. The leftie from New Zealand didn't miss from that distance and the birdie gave him yet another title. Charles' winning score was 274; Nicklaus' was 276. Australian Bruce Crampton took third place one shot behind Nicklaus.

The big hitting American, who is noted for his sportsmanship, praised Charles: "I thought I played pretty well and putted better than I have been for some time, but Bob played better than I did. Bob has always putted well and I think he putts better than anyone on the tour".

Prior to the tournament the championship greens had given problems and when play got under way, many of the competitors had difficulty handling them, but Charles had no trouble with them.

Halfway through the 72 hole event, the Canadian George Knudson was in front, and Canadian supporters were looking for victory. After 54 holes, Charles' putter came into its own.

Nicklaus was a threat in the final round, but Charles managed to hold him off and claim victory.

1968 Canadian Open scoreboard

Total	Name	Scores
274	Bob Charles	70, 68, 70, 66
276	Jack Nicklaus	73, 68, 68, 67
277	Bruce Crampton	71, 68, 72, 66
279	Tommy Aaron	70, 72, 67, 70
279	R. H. Sikes	69, 71, 69, 70
279	Sam Snead	71, 72, 68, 68
279	Tom Weiskopf	69, 71, 69, 70
280	Billy Casper	69, 71, 69, 71
280	Jack Montgomery	75, 71, 69, 65

Piccadilly World Match Play 1969

The putting stroke that had taken Charles to victory in Canada in the summer of 1968 was to show its brilliance once again in the autumn of 1969 on the Wentworth course near London where seven years earlier he had shown a liking for the greens when he tied with Dai Rees for first place in the Daks tournament.

After annihilating Englishman Maurice Bembridge by six and five on the first day and an opening 18 holes of 65 in the 36 hole match he had to be as good on the second day if he was to make the final. He beat Tommy Aaron of the United States nine and seven after going through the halfway mark only one up.

The New Zealander was in the final, playing against American Gene Littler, who like Charles was somewhat controversial. Neither was a 1969 major championship winner and they were playing in a tournament where invitations were extended on the basis of current championship successes.

But Charles had earned the right to play, with second placings in the 1968 and 1969 British Open, runner-up in the 1968 World Match Play and 1968 Canadian Open winner. Littler's invitation had been extended because of the excellence of his United States form in the months preceding the World Match Play.

The New Zealander, who had been ill during the earlier rounds was feeling no better on the morning of the final. Several days of soup and crackers with aspirin and stomach powders was not the type of diet to give a man the energy to play at least 36 holes of match play golf.

The opening 18 holes were tight. Charles held the lead at first; then Littler fought back. The players were all square after 18 of the 36 holes.

Mark McCormack described what happened next: "Immediately after lunch Charles provided a surprise — he three putted a Wentworth green. He then birdied the fifth to get even again; but then three putted once more. That, however, was his last mistake on a green. At the eighth he hit a thin 2 iron into the fairway and an indifferent 4 iron that skittered past the right hand trap and barely made the green. He was 35 feet (11 metres) from the hole with a five foot break over a ridge and he sank it. At the next he made a 30 footer (9 metres) and at the next he chipped into the cup from 45 feet (14 metres). With that one, Charles, who I believe has the least emotional temperament in golf, had to raise his head to the sky. He was now two up."

Charles lost the 13th with a bad drive and Littler who all day had been pumping his approaches into the heart of the greens was not able to get his putter working.

When it seemed the title was Charles', the American got a birdie from 6 feet (2 metres) at the 16th (34th) to bring the match back to square. The next hole was halved.

Mark McCormack describes what happened at the 36th hole: "Littler hit two immaculate wood shots to the fringe of the green, but Charles hooked his second into the trees. It came bounding down, about 120 yards [110 metres] from the green. Charles had a shot and he pitched to exactly 27 feet [8 metres] from the cup. Littler, meantime, ran his approach putt stone dead. Charles stood over his ball and rolled it into the hole as though it was a 2-footer [60 centimetres] on a practice green, Littler shook his head in amazement and the match went into extra holes."

Only one extra hole was needed, Charles putting his second, a No. 4 iron, only 30 inches (76 centimetres) from the pin. Littler left himself a long putt and missed.

McCormack later described Charles' victory as a gutsy performance.

Plenty of critics were quick to say that the better man lost. But Littler himself congratulated Bob on his win, saying that Charles had holed more yardage of putts today than anyone else in the history of golf. "He must be the best putter in the world," said Littler.

Bob and his wife Verity display the Piccadilly World Match Play trophy, London 1969.

During the presentation, Charles said, "I suppose I have some reputation as a putter, and I think I probably maintained it today."

Every golfer learns that you *drive* for show, but *putt* for dough.

PICCADILLY SCOREBOARD

WENTWORTH GOLF CLUB — WEST COURSE

Virginia Water, Surrey October 9-11

Purse . . . £18,400

Par: 534 534 444—36; 345 435 455—38—74

6,997 yards

QUARTER-FINALS

Gary Player (South Africa) defeated Jean Garaialde (France), 10 and 9.

Player
Out: 435 424 445—35
In: 244 435 445—35—70
Garaialde
Out: 445 444 444—37
In: 354 525 555—39—76
Player 5 up
Player
Out: 524 434 444—34
Garaialde
Out: 535 534 554-39

Gene Littler (U.S.) defeated Ray Floyd (U.S.), 6 and 5.

Littler
Out: 324 533 454—33
In: 343 334 455—34—67
Floyd
Out: 434 424 445-34
In: 344 434 455-36-70
Littler 3 up
Littler
Out: 545 433 334-34
In: 334 4
Floyd
Out: 534 633 444—36
In: 345 4

Bob Charles (New Zealand) defeated Maurice Bembridge (UK), 6 and 5.

Bembridge
Out: 435 434 534—35
In: 345 435 454—37—72
Charles
Out: 334 434 444—33
In: 244 324 454—32—65
Charles 7 up
Bembridge
Out: 444 423 545—35
In: 443 4
Charles
Out: 425 434 444—34
In: 445 4

Tommy Aaron (U.S.) defeated Tony Jacklin (U.K.), 6 and 4.

Jacklin
Out: 446 534 344—37
In: 344 434 4C4—X—X
Aaron
Out: 435 534 444—36
In: 344 534 4W4—X—X
Aaron 1 up
Jacklin
Out: 434 544 434—35
In: 344 43
Aaron
Out: 543 434 433—33
In: 334 32

SEMI-FINALS

Littler defeated Player, 4 and 3.

Player
Out: 534 534 434—35
In: 343 424 544—33—68
Littler
Out: 544 533 333—33
In: 334 434 344—32—65
Littler 2 up
Player
Out: 534 544 344—36
In: 344 434
Littler
Out: 434 534 344—34
In: 344 434

Charles defeated Aaron, 9 and 7.

Charles
Out: 424 433 344—31
In: 344 434 445—35—66
Aaron
Out: 435 424 344—33
In: 344 434 444—34—67
Charles 1 up
Charles
Out: 434 424 334—31
In: 33
Aaron
Out: 535 534 445—38
In: 34

FINALS

Charles defeated Littler, 1 up, 37 holes.

Littler
Out: 436 534 445—38
In: 344 434 444—34—72
Charles
Out: 435 524 435—35
In: 344 544 445—37—72
Match even.
Littler
Out: 434 534 444—35
In: 344 434 354—34—69

Charles
Out: 534 524 533—34
In: 244 534 454—35—69

Match even

37th Hole: Charles 3, Littler 4.

Charles received £5,750,;Littler £3,450; Player and Aaron £2,300; Garaialde, Floyd, Bembridge, Jacklin £1,150.

LEGEND: W — won hole; C — conceded hole to opponent; X — no total score.

Air New Zealand Shell — 1978

The Titirangi Golf Course in the western suburbs of Auckland, New Zealand, was not among his favourites. In 1962 it had caused Charles pain in the New Zealand Open championship as torrential rain wreaked havoc.

By 1978 he had put that memory behind him when he went back there for the Air New Zealand Shell Open which was the richest New Zealand event. It was also very well organised.

The presence of Arnold Palmer gave the tournament considerable status. The great American pulled in the crowds. It may have been the enthusiasm of the galleries that got the adrenalin pumping through him faster than he had experienced for years.

After a steady opening round of 67, five under par, Charles was satisfied to be one shot behind Australian Jack Newton. But he felt he would have scored better if they had moved at a reasonable pace.

He partnered Palmer and Peter Thomson of Australia in what should have been an enjoyable round. It wasn't. They took five hours to complete their round because there were a lot of slow players up ahead. It was difficult to keep the momentum going. Charles likes the flow of play to be continuous and not stop and start all the time as they had to that day.

Things were better in the second round. After an indifferent start, with missed birdie putts on the first and second holes and a bogey five at the third he was starting to feel a little down. But then Arnold and Peter canned long birdie putts on the par-three fourth. He was bunkered and came out about 14 feet (5.5 metres) from the hole. Charles relates, "All of a sudden I thought, if they can do it, I can do it. I couldn't afford to drop another shot. I drilled my putt right at the middle of the hole and never missed one after that. That was the turning point for me as I strung together consecutive birdies at the next four holes from 7, 20, 17 and 24 feet (2, 6, 5 and 7.5 metres). Naturally I was feeling good and continued to roll them in on the back nine for a course round of 64, six under par."

Palmer, too, played well but he couldn't match the putting of Charles.

"I played better today than yesterday",

Air New Zealand Shell Scoreboard

Total	Name	Scores
273	Bob Charles (NZ)	67, 64, 73, 69
274	Graham Marsh (Aust)	71, 69, 66, 68
278	Arnold Palmer (USA)	72, 68, 69, 69
278	David Graham (Aust)	67, 67, 74, 70
279	Kel Nagle (Aust)	69, 72, 69, 69
280	Vance Heafner (USA)	67, 71, 74, 68
280	Bob Shaw (USA)	70, 73, 68, 69
280	Rodger Davis (Aust)	70, 67, 71, 72
281	Stewart Ginn (Aust)	69, 67, 72, 73
281	Simon Owen (NZ)	71, 69, 70, 71
281	Bob Shearer (Aust)	70, 72, 68, 71
281	Marty Bohen (USA)	70, 72, 71, 68
282	Robb McNaughton (Aust)	70, 69, 73, 70
282	Paul Firmstone (Aust)	69, 69, 72, 72
282	Scott Simpson (USA)	73, 69, 72, 68
282	Mike Krantz (USA)	71, 69, 68, 74
283	Bob Risch (USA)	67, 69, 77, 70
283	Kurt Cox (USA)	73, 71, 68, 71
283	Bill Dunk (Aust)	73, 72, 71, 67
283	Peter Senior (Aust)	72, 71, 69, 71
283	Mark Lye (USA)	71, 70, 70, 72
283	Rafe Botts (USA)	68, 69, 76, 70

Sensing victory in the 1978 Air New Zealand Shell Open at Titirangi, Auckland, New Zealand. Charles' great approach shot finished close to the pin but despite the distance he took plenty of time to study the line before holing out for victory. *Evening Post*

said Palmer. "But Bob made all the putts — he didn't leave any for us."

With a three shot lead going into the third round, all the pressure was on the New Zealander. A strong wind blowing up late in the day affected his game. A 73 on his card clearly disappointed him, but he was still two shots in front of West Australian Graham Marsh.

Steady rather than spectacular play saw him still in front with seven holes of the last round to play.

As Charles stood on the 14th with a No. 2 iron in his hand he was aware of the thousands of eyes watching his every move. He hit the club — not his favourite, and came right off the shot. The ball hit pine trees on the left of the fairway and dropped into an unplayable lie.

He put down another ball, and managed to do almost exactly the same thing. He finished the hole with a triple bogey six. He really thought he had blown it.

Marsh, playing half an hour ahead of Charles had gone to a two shot lead as he teed off at the last hole. A good tee shot and a well placed pitch into the green had him 18 feet (6 metres) from the pin on the par four hole, but then he blew it, three putting to give Charles, three holes back in the field, the chance of still tieing and forcing a play off.

At the final hole, the left-hander was level with Marsh. A par four would mean a play off. A birdie would give Charles a win. He placed his tee shot within a yard or two of where he wanted it. Then quickly proceeded to toss up a wedge to within 18 in. (50 cm) of the pin. The crowd roared; Charles acknowledged the acclamation and made no mistake with the putt.

Victory was his with a seven under par score of 273 with rounds of 67, 64, 73 and 69. A delighted Charles was back on the victory rostrum.

Tallahassee Open 1983

Early in 1983, Charles and his friend Gary Player dined together in the United States. Talk got round to whether the former British Open champions, both then 47, had to accept that their days of victory were over. Charles said, "We agreed that we could not see anyone on the tour over the age of 45 who had a chance of winning any longer."

Within weeks, Charles had won the Tallahassee Open and as they had done in the 1950s, the 1960s and in the 1970s, writers and commentators raved over the left-hander's victory.

"A Left Wing Organisation?" headlined the mass circulation American golf magazine, *Golf World*. "The new tournament Players' series does not have any political affiliation, but after two events only Southpaws have been victorious, the latest being New Zealand veteran, Bob Charles, who won the Tallahassee Open."

Writer Paul Smith said, "Power to the left-handers, right on."

Charles said, "I was kind of thinking about how a left-hander had won at Magnolia [two weeks earlier]. When we started the final round, I told my caddie, Russ Stieb, 'Let's make it two in a row for left-handers'."

Tallahassee was Charles' first victory in three years, although he had played well in Europe over several seasons.

For a player who hates the wind, Charles produced some excellent mid-tournament golf with rounds of 68 and 67 on the second and third days played in poor weather, to be nine under par for the middle 36 holes. His 72 hole aggregate of 282 tied him with local hero, Greg Powers.

1983 Tallahassee, Florida Open Scoreboard

Total	Name	Scores
282	Bob Charles (New Zealand)	74, 68, 67, 73
282	Greg Powers (USA)	70, 70, 70, 72
Play-off: Charles 3; Powers 4		
283	Mark Lye (USA)	69, 75, 71, 73
283	Kenny Knox (USA)	70, 71, 71, 71
284	Hubert Green (USA)	70, 73, 71, 70
284	Allen Miller (USA)	68, 74, 70, 72
284	Mike Morley (USA)	72, 68, 70, 74
284	Terry Snodgrass (USA)	69, 70, 71, 74
285	Beau Baugh (USA)	73, 70, 68, 74
285	Buddy Gardner (USA)	71, 72, 69, 73
285	Vic Tortorici (USA)	68, 70, 70, 77
286	Lee Elder (USA)	72, 71, 73, 70
286	Bill Kratzert (USA)	69, 77, 69, 71
286	Gary Pinns (USA)	71, 71, 71, 73
286	Rex Caldwell (USA)	69, 69, 73, 75
286	Jeff Mitchell (USA)	68, 69, 71, 78

On the first hole of the sudden death play off, Powers hit his drive down the middle of the fairway, then pushed an iron to the back left edge of the green, just in the rough.

Charles meanwhile was behind a sand trap with his tee shot. His second reached the front left edge of the green, about 50 feet (16 metres) from the hole. The left-hander studied the putting line carefully before stroking it firmly into the hole.

"I was a little disappointed in my second shot. With the putt, I was just trying to get it close, really. But it went straight as an arrow — right into the hole," said Charles later.

Thirty years on — the still-classical swing in evidence at the 1984 Broadbank New Zealand Open. *Evening Post*

In posting rounds of 74, 68, 67, 73 for a 72 hole aggregation of 282, six under par, Charles made some spectacular putts — some for eagles, one for the tournament win and some to save par. During the final round he was in trouble on the fourth hole, a par four named the "Green Monster". His third shot only just made the green, about 60 feet (19 metres) from the hole. "That one was even further than the play off putt," said Charles, "but it was just as important. When I sank that one, it got me par and it helped me pick up my game. I don't think I hit a bad shot after that."

After the amazing putt on the fourth, Charles ran off 10 pars in 11 tries and birdied the other. It took a 9 foot (3 metre) putt on the par three 8th hole to get that birdie, and it took several 15 footers (five metre putts) along the way to save par.

The Tallahassee triumph was his 43rd victory.

"Generally, my putting, when I am confident, is as good as anyone's," said Charles as he folded his cheque for US$36,000.

When he crossed the Atlantic a few weeks later to play the European circuit for the sixth year, Charles spoke with pride of his form at Tallahassee: "Quite unexpected. It gave me some excitement. I thought winning was in the past. I have never won a tournament outside New Zealand without my wife being with me. With Verity there, I'm more relaxed. On my own, I get lonely and miserable. In Florida, I had the whole family along — Verity and my children, Beverley and David. It was great."

The Tallahassee victory was something of a turn around for the left-hander. On the greens he averaged 29 putts for each round, compared with an average of 31 through the 1982 tournaments.

"If I could do better than 30 every week, I could be in contention more often. Putting is basically a state of mind. If I think I am going to miss, I will. If I think I am going to hole it, I'll hole it."

Charles is sure you can talk yourself into a negative state of mind or a positive state of mind.

Chapter Fourteen

Reflections

ALL golfers have their favourite course or courses and I'm no different. Strangely, my top three layouts are courses on which I have never won a major championship in nearly 25 years of tournament play.

I like a lot of courses, but my number one is Pebble Beach in California which has been described by players, writers, broadcasters and professional photographers as probably the most spectacular golf course in the western hemisphere, if not in the world.

Situated on Monterey Peninsula, about 120 miles (190 kilometres) south of San Francisco, Pebble Beach is in perhaps the most sought after real estate area in the United States.

For any golf course to be great it must be like a prize winning cake with excellent ingredients and good presentation. Pebble Beach is just that, with a good variety of holes, a test of golf which never allows one to relax and beautiful scenery.

The 4th, 6th, 7th, 9th, 10th, 17th and 18th holes at Pebble Beach are set along the shoreline of Carmel Bay. These holes have captured the imagination of players, spectators and the millions of people who annually watch the closing stages of the Bing Crosby tournament. The inside holes have also been praised by many players including Jack Nicklaus.

Unfortunately, I've never played well at Pebble Beach. Indeed, I don't recall ever breaking par. But I always enjoy playing there. All the holes are challenging with enough variation to quickly take one's mind off a previous hole played badly. For me the 7th, perhaps the shortest 110 yards (100 metres) in championship golf, is my favourite, especially when played from the elevated tee into a well bunkered green surrounded by surf pounding loudly on the rocky foreshore.

I recall playing the Bing Crosby on one occasion with a chap, who in gale conditions first hit a No. 2 iron into this little hole, only to see the ball fly skywards to be lost forever in the big blue Pacific Ocean. Two further No. 4 irons were hit before my partner finally got down in 10, seven over par, on his way to an even 100 which is a great cricket score. It was the first time I had ever played with a guy who shot 100, but in the conditions I could only feel sorry for him. Pebble Beach in a violent mood is not a happy bed-fellow.

My second course also sits on the seashore. It is St Andrews in Scotland, certainly my favourite layout among those used for the British Open although I have never won there.

Naturally, I also have an affection for Royal Lytham and St Annes on the Lancashire Coast where I won my most prestigious title, the 1963 British Open. That affection is reflected in my naming my farm at Oxford in Canterbury, Lytham.

St Andrews is unique in golf with its seven double greens, its bunkers and its ever changing moods brought about by bitter winds blowing in from the North Sea. It plays either too long or too short and at most times the fairways are fiery — the ball is subject to erratic bounce. Despite my dislike of wind, I just can't go past St Andrews as a great golf course. I love it and I feel at home with the local people who follow the big tournaments. Their knowledge and understanding of the history of the game make them special among the hundreds of thousands of people who tread the fairways of the world's courses watching the professionals at work.

In spite of my inability to score well on its manicured fairways and slick greens, I place Augusta, home of the famed United States Masters, as number three on my ranking list.

I played in the Masters 15 times, mainly with disappointing results, but I enjoyed those annual visits to this unique event which is always played on the same course at the same time of the year (always early April) and under the same conditions with the exception of the weather which is fickle to say the least.

There is nothing strange about my choosing as tops three courses on which I've never won events. I like Pebble Beach, St Andrews and Augusta, the surroundings, the atmosphere and the thought that perhaps one day I might return to those courses and leave satisfied.

Away from the pressures of those courses, I do have a love and respect for two fine layouts in the South Pacific — Royal Melbourne in Australia and Paraparaumu Beach near Wellington, New Zealand.

The composite course at Royal Melbourne is the pride of the many sandbelt courses in Australia's second biggest city and is, in my view, among the best inland layouts in the world. It features wide fairways, many heavily trapped or doglegged which generally favour long hitters. But the key to real success on this course is an ability to be able to read the slick greens and putt well.

About 1,200 miles (2,000 kilometres) across the Tasman Sea is Wellington, renowned for its wind. Thirty miles (50 kilometres) north is the Paraparaumu Beach links where over the years I have enjoyed many successes. While those victories have certainly made me feel at home on the undulating fairways and greens of Paraparaumu, I have long held the view that this course rates as New Zealand's best because of the winds which in the space of a few minutes can transform it from a comparatively straightforward course to a demanding test which requires 100 per cent dedication to every shot if good scoring is to result.

Looking to the future

All things progress and with progress comes change. Nowhere is that more evident in the game of golf than in the United States. The United States PGA tour has grown like Topsy. With that growth has come the need for something new.

In 1983, a new tour was started in the United States of America to provide competition for those who were not playing the PGA events. Known as the Tournament Players' Series, the 1983 programme provided 10 events and prize money of US$2,000,000. A year later more events were added and the prize money was increased. I was eligible for the TPS series and took out the Tallahassee Open. Through 1984 and into 1985, I played more TPS events and now, as I plan for my 50th birthday, I can look forward to the other exciting innovation in American golf — the Seniors' Tour, which is for players 50 years of age and over.

The growth of this tour has been dramatic since it started at the beginning of the 1980s. Its success has been due to the charisma of the players — Arnold Palmer, Gene Littler, Doug Sanders, Miller Barber, Australian Peter Thomson and many more outstanding tournament players from the 1950s, 1960s and 1970s. I think the personalities of many of the seniors has helped to make this tour so popular with spectators. Many who follow the players on course or in their homes through television, are age contemporaries of those players even if they could not match their abilities as strikers of the golf ball.

The Seniors' tour has a big advantage over the other tours in the fact that the money is guaranteed. All players who tee up for a Seniors' tournament are guaranteed a pay-packet before they strike their first drive. There is prize money on top of that.

This is, of course, exciting and certainly eases the mental strain. Very rarely during my many years on the PGA tour and elsewhere was I given a guarantee before teeing off.

To be playing every week with guaranteed prize money has just got to be the greatest way to play the game. It's like getting a pension years before you are entitled to it!

That, among other things, is why I have been looking forward to my 50th birthday.

Caddies

No professional golfer can really function effectively without a caddy.

Over the years, I've had the good fortune to employ caddies who have contributed greatly to my successes in the game.

Among the many enjoyable young kids and older characters who have carried for me, I should mention Emet Smith (Smithy). For 10 years in the United States, including our first event together as a team — the 1963 Houston Classic, which I won — he looked after my clubs and was a great companion and ally as we moved back and forth to tournaments.

My association of 22 years with Frank Gilmore in the United Kingdom was another warm and rewarding relationship.

Frank was unique among caddies for the very reason that he did not use yardages (metres) as do modern caddies.

He relied on his experience, his knowledge of the courses we played and excellent eyesight which enabled him to help in correct club selection with rewarding results, my 1963 British Open win being just one example of Frank's true worth.

There have been numerous others, including Michael Glading, son of a life-long friend Bob Glading, a past winner of the New Zealand Open Championship. Caddies, especially the right guys, can make — or break — a player. I count myself fortunate to have had a rewarding association with this dedicated and hard-working breed.

Appendix

My major victories

Major Tournaments Won.

New Zealand
New Zealand Open championship — 1954 (as an amateur); 1966, 1970 and 1973
New Zealand Professional Golfers' Association championship — 1961, 1978, 1979 and 1980
Auckland City Classic — 1974
Air New Zealand Shell Open — 1978

In addition Charles won a number of other important events through the 1960s and 1970s under the sponsorship of numerous trading and commercial houses.

United States
Houston Classic — 1963
Tucson Open — 1965
Atlanta Classic — 1967
Greater Greensboro Open — 1974
Tallahassee Open — 1983

Canada
Canadian Open — 1968

Great Britain
British Open — 1963
World Match Play championship — 1969
Dunlop Masters — 1972
John Player Classic — 1972

Europe and Scandinavia
Swiss Open — 1962 and 1974
Scandinavian Open — 1974

South Africa
South African Open — 1973

* During his years on the US tour, Charles was in the Elite 60 during the following years — 1963-1965; 1967-1971 and again in 1974. His best year on the US tour was in 1967 when he won US$72,468 for 11th placing on the money ladder.

* When his main sphere of activity switched to Britain and Europe during the 1970s, he finished in the top 10 on the Order of Merit ladder on five occasions.

* His winning score of 261 (67, 63, 64 and 67) in winning the New Zealand Professional Golfers' Association title in 1979 was the lowest four round score for any New Zealand major tournament.

BOB CHARLES AT WORK